Teaching 201

Traveling Beyond the Basics

LINDA HENSHALL WILSON

ScarecrowEducation
Lanham, Maryland • Toronto • Oxford
2004

Published in the United States of America
by ScarecrowEducation
An imprint of The Rowman & Littlefield Publishing Group, Inc.
4501 Forbes Boulevard, Suite 200, Lanham, Maryland 20706
www.scaroweducation.com

PO Box 317
Oxford
OX2 9RU, UK

Copyright © 2004 by Linda Henshall Wilson

British Library Cataloguing in Publication Information Available

Library of Congress Cataloging-in-Publication Data

Wilson, Linda Henshall, 1952–
  Teaching 201 : traveling beyond the basics / Linda Henshall Wilson.
    p. cm.
  Includes bibliographical references.
  ISBN 1-57886-064-4 (pbk. : alk. paper)
  1. First-year teachers—Handbooks, manuals, etc. 2.
Teachers—Professional relationships—Handbooks, manuals, etc. I.
Title: Teaching two hundred one. II. Title.
LB2844.1.N4 W57 2004
371.1—dc21
                                                    2003010011

∞™ The paper used in this publication meets the minimum requirements of
American National Standard for Information Sciences—Permanence of
Paper for Printed Library Materials, ANSI/NISO Z39.48-1992.
Manufactured in the United States of America.

With love to my first and favorite teachers, my parents, Ray and Peggy Henshall, and my sister Carol. Continue to nurture!

With love to my favorite student, my son, Scott. Continue to soar!

With love to my husband, Allan. Continue to encourage!

With love to my students past, present, and future. Continue to be spectacular!

With appreciation and gratitude to all my former teachers—at church, at public school, at the higher education level.

With respect and admiration to those who teach with passion, dedication, and joy so all students will learn. Continue to let your light shine brightly in your classrooms throughout our nation!

Contents

Introduction

Congratulations! The doors of opportunity have opened wide and you have entered into the realm of "school." You have been given the opportunity to become a teacher. Your potential for success is unlimited.

The purpose of this book is to provide novice and seasoned teachers alike with guidelines for success during their careers. This is not a survival guide. Setting the goal of survival is too low a mark of achievement for you. This book will take you far beyond the gauge of survival into the area of success. Why tread water when you can win an Olympic medal in swimming? This book will help you become a medallist, one of the top contenders in the field of education. Your dogpaddling days are over. Imagine yourself standing on the podium with a medal around your neck and the national anthem playing. With the help of this book, you will surpass survival and become a confident, focused, effective, and successful professional.

This book was Teaching 101. After several chapters, I realized that this was not a basic book with information that you would receive at an entry or beginning level—the 101 level. This was going to include "extras"—suggestions, web references for further thinking, pearls of wisdom, and much more. This book title should be Teaching 201—a higher-level title for a higher-level book.

I originally wanted to title this book The Journey from Teacher to Professional: The Nuts, Sprinkles, Whipped Cream, and Cherry. This book contains the extras—from small suggestions to powerful pearls of wisdom—that most likely are not included in the standard teacher education classes or in a student teaching experience. As a teacher, you will see colleagues who simply have their acts together in an outstanding way. They are very well organized, they spend little time on the trivialities of teaching, and they always seem to have a "plan B" if "plan A" fails. These colleagues are not just teachers; they are true professionals. This book will assist you by providing ideas and options for management (which I refer to as daily housekeeping tasks), communicating among and between a myriad of individuals, planning, assessment, and (most important) meeting student needs.

In one of my doctoral courses, we spent several class sessions discussing the profound issue of teaching: Was teaching an art, a science, or a craft? While the other students in the class eagerly debated this topic, I wanted to add a fourth category: a journey. I believe that teaching parallels a journey much more closely than it corresponds to an art, a science, or a craft. I see the experiences of teachers paralleling those of an individual taking a journey in the following ways:

- Teachers plan each day thoroughly to ensure the best learning experiences possible for the students. People taking a journey plan extensively to make the most of their trip. If you fail to plan, you plan to fail!
- Teachers' days are filled with the "unexpected." A journey also has those little unexpected joys and wonderful surprises that suddenly appear. No matter how well we prepare for a journey, roadblocks, setbacks, and detours always occur.
- Teachers have the opportunity to meet fascinating individuals of all ages, races, genders, and faiths. Even if classrooms are filled with "tracked" students of similar academic abilities, working every day with a variety of individuals is a heterogeneous experience. Each student is unique with his or her own gifts, talents, intelligences, strengths, and weaknesses. Life is also heterogeneous, and individuals making a journey, especially, meet a myriad of individuals.

Throughout our lives, we make a series of journeys. These journeys may be personal, professional, emotional, or spiritual. Many individuals believe that life itself is a journey. The journey discussed throughout this book is a professional one.

A journey has a point or place of departure. Each intended reading group for this book has its own departure location. For the teacher education major, your departure into the realm of teaching may occur when you begin making classroom observations or your first day of student teaching. For the practicing teacher, it may be the very first day of school as a teacher with your own classroom and students. For the alternative certification candidate, the point of departure into teaching may be when you decided to pursue your dream and make it a reality. Your departure may have begun when you signed your teaching contract. Each group or individual *did* have a departure point into the professional journey.

To best assist the reader, I have a "Road Map" at the beginning of each chapter. The road map explains where each of the intended readers should begin reading the chapter. Time is a valuable commodity not to be wasted. I considered the reader's valuable time when designing the chapters. For example, some chapters may have parts that could be considered "review" for individuals who have completed a teacher education program at the university level. This same information is invaluable to the individual who has become a teacher through the alternative certification route.

Just as a journey has a point of departure, it also has a destination location. For some educators, the destination is retirement. For me, the destination is attaining the highest level of professionalism possible. Abraham Maslow constructed a hierarchy of needs in which the uppermost realm is referred to as "self-actualization." This self-actualization is my professional destination—ultimate professionalism.

My husband spent the vast majority of his personal and professional life either playing or coaching baseball. He often spoke of a player who was in a "slump"—no matter how many adjustments coaches made with his hitting style, the player just couldn't seem to be a productive hitter. To someone in a batting slump, the ball looks like a pea or a tiny ball bearing coming at them. The other end of the continuum is the baseball player who is "in the groove"—someone who can hit any ball thrown over the plate—a change-up, a curveball, a slider, a heater—this individual can hit *anything*. It seems as if the baseball is the size of a cantaloupe. To baseball players, it is hitting in the groove; to followers of Maslow, it is attaining the level of self-actualization; to practicing teachers, it is achieving ultimate professionalism.

As professional educators, the destination of "professionalism" is attainable. We have planned and prepared with great care and effort. Our teaching practices are grounded in "good practice" applications. Our days in the classroom are enjoyable rather than tense and stressed. Our positive experience overflows to the students. Because we are enjoying our time as teachers, the students have a much more enjoyable and productive time in their educational experiences. This is "education in the groove."

We have discussed the departure and the destination, but what is the journey? I believe that the journey is a continuum. Individual teachers are interspersed at different points along the continuum, depending on where they are specifically located on *their* professional journey. Just as every individual has a different span on life's journey, educators have an individualized length of time along their professional journeys.

It is the intent of this book to supply readers with information that will move them farther and faster along the professional continuum; therefore, I added the second part of the title, *Traveling Beyond the Basics*. After completing the reading of this book, the reader will be able to move away from the basics—or the beginning point on the continuum—to a position closer to the destination.

WHY I WROTE THIS BOOK

Throughout my educational career, I have had the opportunity to be a "professional gypsy." I taught self-contained elementary grades 2, 3, 4, 5, and 6. I also taught a combined third and fourth grade class (today known as "multi-age") at a small rural school. I've also been a "special" teacher teaching elementary music and Indian heritage. My career has extended to junior high (now called middle school), high school, undergraduate-level teacher education courses, and graduate-level courses. My teaching experiences have ranged from running off those old purple dittos to conducting interactive telecourses. I have over twenty years of practical teaching experience as well as a doctorate degree in educational administration with a study emphasis in school district leadership. I understand the role of the classroom teacher, the role of the administrator, and the role of the teacher education professor. As Scott's mother, I understand the parental point of view from kindergarten through high school. I am able to view education from several vantage points.

Reason 1

As a university professor, I have had the privilege to work with many first-year elementary, middle school, and high school teachers as their university representative. I quickly discovered that the first-year teachers generally asked the *same questions*. I was spinning my wheels repeating the same explanations year after year. After much frustration and soul-searching, I have compiled my pearls of wisdom in this book to attempt to answer those continuously asked questions. The areas targeted are universal to teaching: management or daily housekeeping tasks, communication among and between a myriad of individuals, planning, assessment, and (most importantly) meeting student needs.

If the individuals whom I was supervising seemed to be asking the same questions year after year, could individuals across the country be wondering about the same issues? These questions were ordinary, commonsense garden-variety questions. I have used them as the framework for this book. The contents will assist you in maintaining your classroom as well as your sanity. I have included some suggestions and ideas that are one of a kind, totally unique to the world of educational writing. Rather than reading the "rocket science of teaching," my specialty is "common sense from professional experience." Rather than advising you to move to an ivory tower perspective, I prefer to suggest experiences from the trenches. As Billy Graham once said, the harvest comes from the valley rather than from the mountaintop. We teach in the valleys of education every day rather than from the mountaintops.

I have also had the opportunity to work with educators who have sought alternative certification; that is, they did not become an educator through the traditional teacher education route. Alternative certification teachers are also referred to as midcareer teachers. They have already had one career and now have chosen to meet all requirements to become a certified teacher. In 2002, forty-one states in the United States recognized alternative certification teachers. The alternative certification teachers with whom I worked had the same types of questions as those who had come from teacher education programs. If the alternative certification teachers and the teachers coming from teacher education backgrounds have the *same questions*, perhaps those questions should be formally addressed in a book.

Reason 2

I have tremendous admiration and confidence in the individuals whom I have worked with in our teacher education program. I expect them to stay in the profession from their graduation till they become eligible for retirement. Having high expectations is wonderful; however, looking at my students and students nationally from a realistic perspective, not all of these individuals will remain in the profession. Nationwide, more than one-fifth of classroom teachers in U.S. public schools leave their positions within the first three years of public school teaching, according to the National Center for Educational Statistics in 1992. Authorities have estimated teacher attrition ratios in the first five years to be between 30 and 50 percent.

Every parent has made the statement "not my child" when the issue of misconduct arises. All parents believe that *their* child would not do such a thing. I feel the same way about my university students. *My* teacher education candidates would not become part of the national statistics—*not my students!* Sadly, even some of my former students will someday drop out of the rank and file of America's educators.

I do not want my teacher education students to become a part of these statistics. I do not want any teacher to leave the profession. It is my sincere desire to provide information that will best assist the reader not just to remain in the profession but to move along the continuum to attain ultimate professionalism.

Reason 3

If we can accept the previous statistics from the National Center for Educational Statistics, then the burning question "Why?" arises. These are individuals who have "been called" to become teachers, endured the rigors of teacher education programs across the country, and struggled and persevered mightily to attain their first job in the profession (the first job is always the most difficult to attain!). Yet for one reason or another, national statistics reveal that one in every five teachers leaves the profession within the first three years. Why? No solid, concrete, set-in-stone rationale comes to the forefront. It is my educated opinion (a tactful way of stating a guess without reputable research to back up the statement) that the reasons could be classified in one of two categories: (1) management and/or (2) instructional strategies.

One-fifth of this book is devoted to the topic of management or daily housekeeping tasks. You have heard the expression "Don't sweat the small stuff." In the teaching profession the small stuff will eat you alive. Proper planning, proper preparedness, and attempting to have a plan B somewhere up your sleeve can eliminate much frustration from your days in the classroom. This book attempts to share pearls of wisdom to best assist you in this area.

Three-fifths of this book is devoted to the general topic of teaching or instructional strategies. As an adult learner, you had certain classes in your college experience in which you truly connected with the professor and the subject matter. The key was that this particular professor was not necessarily the best in the west; however, the professor taught to your particular learning style. The contents of this book will take you by the hand and introduce you (or reacquaint you) with the learning styles, modes of learning, and various types of assessment.

Using your basic mathematics skills, you have added one-fifth and three-fifths and have still not come up with one whole. In my training in educational administration, I learned the vital and paramount importance of human relations—the last fifth of the book's contents. As an administrator, human relations can make you or break you. As an elementary teacher studying doctoral educational administration classes in night school, I decided to try out some of these ideas on my parents, administrators, and fellow colleagues. Everyone associated with the education world can benefit from a "human relations makeover." I received rave reviews from appreciative parents who welcomed the opportunity to know *what* their child was learning in school, *when* important events were scheduled, and *how* they could best assist their children from the home perspective.

Reason 4

I have previously explained my rationale for using the metaphor of teaching as a journey. I have discussed the concept of a continuum on which the teachers travel. Teachers don't just grasp the diploma one moment and attain "professional" status the next. This journey takes time. "We have verified that it takes between five to eight years to master the craft of teaching," according to Dr. David Berlinger, dean of the College of Education at Arizona State University ("Improving the Quality of the Teaching Force: A Conversation with David C. Berlinger," Association for Supervision and Curriculum Development, *Educational Leadership* [May 2001]: 7). Berlinger uses the term *master the craft*; I use the term *attain professionalism*. Mastering the craft of teaching is equivalent to moving to the far end of the professional continuum. In baseball terms, it means to hit in the groove.

Putting nomenclature aside, Dr. Berlinger concurs with me on the fact that the multifaceted concept of teaching evolves through practice over time—the continuum, or the journey. Educators do not just master the craft through osmosis. I believe that not just time but also the incorporation of the best teaching practices boosts the educator along the continuum. A student does not pass a course by just attending the class over time. Much more is involved in successful education. The same is true of becoming a professional—traveling beyond the basics. A teacher does not attain the "ultimate professional" status by just showing up for work each day (or "experience" over time).

This elite status is achieved by those who "come to teach." Athletes do not simply arrive for a competition—they have come to win. This attitude is shared by those ultimate professionals as well. I recall a warm, sunny spring day a few years ago. I spoke on the phone with my sister's three-year-old granddaughter. Jenna wanted me to leave school and play with her on the trampoline at her house. I told her that I could not come. I was busy educating America's future leaders. I had "come to teach"—fifth graders, but nonetheless they would someday be America's future leaders.

I have supervised first-year teachers for only a one-year time span. I always see much improvement over the nine-month period. When my time is completed, I move on to work with a different group of individuals the next year. I do not return to see the first-year teachers in their second year or further in their careers. I believe that I would see continual improvements in all aspects of teaching because they will truly improve using good teaching practices over time. Just as a basketball player improves making free throws (using good form) or a hurdler shaves seconds off his or her time (with proper coaching on the fundamentals of running and jumping over a series of hurdles), teachers improve their skills over time. Teachers can use "good form" and "good fundamentals" just as athletes do. "Poor form" could lead to individuals' becoming part of the national statistics of those leaving the profession. This book is filled with suggestions and ideas that are considered best practice in teaching terms.

DESIGN

This book has a unique design. As already mentioned, information is given at the beginning of each chapter to guide the reader. This literary road map informs the three target reading groups as to where to begin reading each chapter. Although my ego would be thrilled to have everyone read every word, practicality and usefulness prevail in this book. Time is a vital element to every individual. Why waste it reading information that will not benefit you? Therefore, I have made every effort to assist the reader by providing a chapter road map.

In keeping with the journey motif, I have designed "Technology Excursion Trips" within the chapters; look for the Technology Excursion icon. These trips follow a chart or table that has been created using Microsoft Word for illustration and further explanation. As a university professor, I learn every day from my technologically gifted students. We are continually sharing suggestions and instructions on how to create better visual graphics. The techniques my students perfect in class can be transposed to other courses as well as utilized when they are classroom teachers. Teacher education candidates can create rubrics or event chains for future university assignments. The practicing teacher can read the chapter today, create the graphic organizer at home tonight, and utilize the new concepts tomorrow with his or her students—immediate implementation. The steps in each Technology Excursion Trip are basic in design. This information in the hands of creative and innovative educators will be helpful, useful, and soon become a part of their daily teaching practice and routine.

At the end of each main part of the book, the reader will find a "Detour" section. The detour provides readers with tips and suggestions to best assist them on their quest to become ultimate professionals. Many of the suggestions are "known" within the profession but rarely described in a university textbook or professional education book. As a university representative supervising first-year teachers and student teachers, I often see situations that could have been easily alleviated through best practice. These best-practice suggestions are simple, well-known strategies that seasoned professionals have honed throughout their careers and that will assist the classroom teacher working today. They will serve as a preview for teacher education candidates who will soon be working on internships, student teaching, or clinical practice assignments. The suggestions will also be helpful to teacher education candidates taking such courses as instructional strategies, evaluations and assessments (tests and measurements), and classroom management. These pearls of wisdom will be helpful to you. Take the time to take the detour.

This book also offers both scholarly and Internet references. You may not have the opportunity or time to use a university library to find further information on a specific subject. Web addresses are provided to allow you to explore an avenue using your own computer at home.

WHO SHOULD READ THIS BOOK?

This book has three sorts of reader in mind: (1) teacher education candidates (college sophomores, juniors, and seniors); (2) current teachers working in public or private schools; and (3) individuals who have attained certification through the alternative certification process and do not have a teacher education background.

Teacher Education Majors

Wherever you are in your career as an educator, this book is for you. If you still have that magnificent gleam in your eye and are currently a teacher education candidate at a prestigious university or college, you will reap many pearls of wisdom from this book. I pray that it will inspire you to yearn for the moment you step into your very own classroom. You will glean practical suggestions and ideas that you can utilize when student teaching or in clinical practice. You will also have a working vocabulary—teacher talk—that will assist you with your supervising teacher and as a novice in the teachers' lounge discussions. This book will give you an "edge" on successful teaching practices.

Alternative Certification Candidates

If you have chosen to become a teacher through the route of alternative certification, this book offers both the basics and beyond for you. You will benefit from the theories from education's finest as well as suggestions for practical use. Your past professional experiences may be very helpful to you in the areas, for example, of communication. You will, however, blend your communication skills with tips for parent–teacher conferences or student-led conferences. Your past experiences will be very helpful to you. This book will help you build an educational structure on top of your present professional foundation.

Alternative certification candidates will also find instructional strategies and classroom management tips that will be very helpful. Also here is the jargon, lingo, or "teacher talk" that frequents teachers' lounges across the country. This book will help you "walk the walk and talk the talk" with confidence, self-assurance, and certainty.

Teachers Presently in the Field

Remember the comment from the esteemed dean of education from Arizona State University? Mastering the craft of teaching evolves over time while using the best practices. This book will refresh your knowledge of the basics of teacher education while providing you with an "enrichment portion." For example, in the chapter "Reporting Grades," you can prepare a supplemental sheet to send home along with the standard progress report. This supplemental sheet will provide you with insight and perspective from both the student and the parents. You can use this as a foundation for student or parent conferences. This is just one example of how you can take information from this book and personalize it to meet the needs of your classroom.

No matter where you are in your school year, you can pick up this book today and put it into practice tomorrow in your classroom. Whether you are just beginning your first year or are a seasoned professional in the middle of your school year, this book is designed to give you ideas, strategies, and insights that you can adapt to meet the needs of your classroom. With less time spent on the trivial happenings in your room, you will have more time to devote to your students. Spending the least amount of time possible on trivialities and still reaping the optimum rewards is what I refer to as "teaching smart."

A strong area of my expertise is in the field of measurements and evaluations —the old tests and measurements class you took in college, but with a performance-based assessment emphasis. This book gives illustrations and examples to create rubrics, checklists, and rating scales. These evaluation instruments can be used by virtually *any* teacher teaching *any* curricular subject. Remember that mental list of fun ways you would like for your students to learn? You can do those things and still have a percentile grade recorded in the grade book or on your computerized grading program. Your administrator will be happy, the parents will be happy, and your kinesthetic learners will be the happiest of all. This is just one topic that you can read about and directly put into practice with your students. The book is filled with such ideas.

MAKING THE TRANSITION: MOVING FROM ONE SIDE OF THE DESK TO THE OTHER

I have the opportunity to work at the same university site in which I was a student for many years. You could say that I have moved from one side of the desk to the other—from the student side to the teacher side. The perspective is much different. Rather than just showing up for class, I now must be completely prepared. If additional supplies are needed, I must purchase them far in advance. If equipment is to be utilized, I must come prior to class to set up the overhead document machine or the computer and have everything ready when the students arrive. There is a huge gap between being a student and becoming a teacher.

Evaluations are much different now. Not only do I evaluate students, but they also evaluate me. My evaluation is important to me for a multiple of reasons. As a student, I had just two or three evaluations per semester in the form of examinations or projects. As a professor, *every* student evaluates me as well as peers/colleagues and also my university superiors. Taking a few tests was much easier than creating the tests from scratch.

As a classroom teacher, you have made that move from one side of the desk to the other. Sometimes you have just a few weeks to make that transition. Although as teachers we still have the wonderful opportunity of continuing to learn every day, we also have to assume the responsibilities associated with our jobs. This book will assist you in grasping the reality of your responsibilities. By reading this book both prior to and also during your teaching experiences, you will be able to become proactive in your quest to meet the needs of your students, your parents, and your faculty as well as attempt to alleviate the unforeseen pitfalls associated with the education profession.

Take a long look at an empty classroom filled with desks and chairs. Think to yourself, "What if . . . ?" Take the contents of this book and make those "what if's" become reality for you. Create a hassle-free conference day. Use those creative topics you have always wanted to include in your repertoire in a way that has a rubric or rating scale to show students' progress and grades for the grade book. Design a personalized planning book that best meets your needs. Think outside the box on your options! As Albert Einstein said, "Creativity is more important than knowledge." As Albert Schweitzer said, "The most important goal of education is to make young people think for themselves." Building on Dr. Schweitzer's statement, I suggest that we encourage and stimulate teachers to think for themselves—outside the box. Begin your journey today!

I

ADDRESSING STUDENT NEEDS

What do we teach students in school? We teach them that two and two make four and that Paris is the capital of France. When will we also teach them what they are? We should say to each of them: Do you know what you are? You are a marvel! . . . In the millions of years that have passed, there has never been another person like you. You could become a Shakespeare, a Michelangelo, a Beethoven. You have the capacity for anything. Yes, you are a marvel!

—*Pablo Casals ("Joys and Sorrows: Reflections by Pablo Casals," On the Beam III 4, no. 101 [April 1983]: 101)*

Every student has strengths and limitations. This section begins with the various learning modalities and then moves on to teaching strategies and the major educational theories. Special needs students are addressed with suggestions for the classroom teacher.

1

Learning Modalities

How Students Learn

School administrators, board of education members, and various community leaders are impressed with student achievement on standardized tests—"what" is learned and marked correctly on a test given for a few minutes one day of the school year. Teachers working with the students on a daily basis want to know "how" the students learn. The various ways or modes of learning are referred to as learning modalities. *This chapter will examine the traditional three learning modalities and also introduce a fourth.*

This chapter will benefit all three intended readerships. Teacher education candidates and alternative certification candidates will benefit from reading about the various learning modalities. The teacher currently in the field will benefit from reading about the fourth learning modality. Look for the heading marked "The Fourth Learning Modality" to find information on the VARK Inventory.

For many years educators have explored the way in which students learn—"how" they learn. Students could be kinesthetic, auditory, or visual learners.

Kinesthetic learners learn by doing. These are the students who love to physically construct things and use manipulatives in *all* subjects. Remember the term "hands-on learning" from your old methods courses? Why not take a hands-on approach in social studies or spelling or any other curricular area? This method of teaching will appeal to the kinesthetic learner.

Auditory learners learn by hearing or listening. The auditory learner benefits from small-group or teacher-led discussions. These students process information auditorily and store it away in mental file cabinets. The auditory learner may not give the teacher eye contact. These children are too busy listening to spend time worrying about direct eye contact. If a class video is shown, these students may not pay much attention but will be able to answer all the questions because they listened so very well. Auditory learners have excellent auditory processing skills. These students benefit from not only hearing the teacher or an audiovisual aid such as a video or DVD but also from hearing other students. Auditory learners thrive in small-group discussions and small-group guided practice assignments.

Visual learners learn by seeing, either from a textbook or from the chalkboard or overhead. These students benefit greatly by seeing the science experiment or seeing the social studies map. You will love visual learners because they *will* give the teacher eye contact. They will watch your every move. Visual learners also benefit from visuals you use in your classroom such as a bulletin board or various charts displayed in the classroom.

When designing lessons for your class, consider lessons that appeal to more than one learning modality. If you bring out the geoboards for a lesson on geometry, geoboards and rubber bands appeal to kinesthetic learners when they manually put the various rubber bands on the pegs to create the angles, triangles, rectangles, or squares. When you ask the students to verbally describe their angles, triangles, rectangles, or squares, this approach will appeal to the auditory learners in your classroom. This same geoboard lesson will appeal to the visual learners who see the various angles, triangles, rectangles, or squares. The use of colored rubber bands will enhance learning for visual learners as well as students in your classroom with some learning problems.

Designing lessons that promote a specific learning modality can benefit your students with learning problems or language proficiency problems. Students with special learning needs will benefit from lessons that appeal to a variety of learning styles. An ESL (English as a second language) or LEP (limited English-proficient) student would be highly frustrated trying to listen to a teacher lecture or trying to take notes in class. Such a learner does not have the language skills to complete this task. Teachers with ESL or LEP students can use the same content in a lesson that appeals to the visual and kinesthetic learners. If you have students with auditory processing problems, again use visual and kinesthetic lessons to help those students learn. Effective teaching will result in effective learning—for all students.

In all subjects, try to find activities for the students that appeal to at least two of the learning modalities. Often the classroom teacher will create a learning environment that utilizes all three learning modalities. In my university methods courses, I refer to this as "hitting a home run" or "batting a thousand" because you have covered all three learning modalities. Balance is the key. Rather than saturating each class period with only a lecture or only manipulatives, create a balance in your lessons throughout each day. Your students will enjoy the balance and variety of learning modality lessons. You will keep your enthusiasm and motivation at a high level with the variety as well.

Know your own learning modality. Teaching styles generally reflect the teacher's learning preference. Thus, teachers design lessons around *their* learning modality—they can teach their modality and disregard the other options. This is a very easy professional trap into which teachers can fall. Think back to your top two or three favorite teachers. Did they teach to your learning modality? Is that perhaps why they were a favorite of yours? Be sensitive to include a variety of lessons throughout each day.

Here are a few websites where you can take a learning style inventory and diagnose your specific learning style:

www.tvi.cc.nm.us/~gbw/learnstyle.html

www.metamath.com/multiple/multiple_choice_questions.cgi

www.geocitiesl.com/~educationplace/1styulelinks.html

www.ldpride.net/learningstyles.MI.htm

www.learnactivity.com/assessment.html

THE FOURTH LEARNING MODALITY

The three learning modalities previously mentioned have been accepted by educators as the standard ways in which students learn. A fourth modality, however, has come to the forefront in recent years. Developed in the late 1980s by Dr. Neil Fleming, the VARK Inventory, which is a mnemonic for visual, auditory, reading/writing, and kinesthetic, was the first learning style inventory to also provide students and educators with practical guidelines for teaching and learning in each of the four areas (Dunn 2001). After completing the VARK Inventory, which can be taken and graded online (www.vark-learn.com), the students are scored in each of the four categories. The higher the score in any one category, the greater the student's ability to acquire knowledge in that mode of delivery. (For more information on the VARK Inventory, visit www.active-learning-site.com/inventory1.html.)

Julia Dunn, who teaches beginning athletic training and advanced athletic training at Whitman College, takes the information from the VARK Inventory to group the students for learning activities. The following is an explanation of utilizing different learning styles to learn about anatomy and injuries of the human knee:

> Based on the students' pre-assessed VARK scores, they were divided into four groups (students with multiple strengths could self-select into one of two groups) and given 15 minutes to review the material. The visual learners took large pieces of butcher paper and drew diagrams of the knee. They labeled important anatomical landmarks, marked frequently injured structures, and drew schematics of how those injuries might occur. The auditory and reading/writing learners worked together. One group wrote as much as they could about the knee in each of the three areas (anatomy, injuries, and mechanisms). The auditory group then read aloud to a partner the paragraphs written by the reading/writing group. Finally each student in the kinesthetic group was given a lump of clay and Popsicle sticks. They built elaborate working knee models. Working in pairs they demonstrated with their models how a certain mechanism might damage a specific structure. (Dunn 2001: 3)

As a university professor, Dunn includes the VARK Inventory as part of the first class meeting. If you wish to try this approach with your students, please do it at the beginning of the school year if possible. What used to take me a few weeks to assess, you will know in a matter of minutes. You can then utilize that information to best assist your students throughout the remainder of the year.

Additional suggestions when using the VARK Inventory: First take the test yourself. Also, consider the age appropriateness of the questions for your students. Younger students cannot read the questions; thus, they cannot take the test. Primary students who have not mastered a large reading and writing vocabulary should avoid taking this test. Older students, however, will enjoy taking the test and realizing ways in which they process and learn new information.

CONCLUSION

Teachers have long examined the question of how students learn. This chapter examined the traditionally accepted three learning modalities—kinesthetic, visual, and auditory—and also introduced a fourth modality—the VARK Inventory. The following two chapters will also examine the question of how students learn. Chapter 2 offers a wealth of teaching strategies to appeal to the diverse learning population in your classroom. Chapter 3 connects these strategies to the various learning theories—connecting practice to theory.

REFERENCE

Dunn, J. L. 2001. Assess learning styles for more effective teaching. *Teaching Professor* 15, no. 5 (June/July 2001): 3.

2

Teaching Strategies to Help Students Learn

This chapter is designed for all three groups of readers. Now that the reader understands "how" students learn, this chapter offers a variety of teaching strategies to best teach the visual, auditory, reading/writing, and kinesthetic learners. The strategies can be adapted for students from preschool (age four) through twelfth grade. Obviously, the early childhood classroom would use the strategies as a class project, with the teacher writing down the information on a large chart or bulletin board. The strategies can be used as either individual or group practice activities. Many of the strategies in this chapter could also be used as a summative assessment over a unit or chapter.

This chapter also provides "Technology Excursion Trips." Step-by-step directions are given for you to create the charts and tables in this chapter. The classroom teacher can read the chapter today, create the visuals tonight, and use them in the classroom tomorrow—the beauty of technology! The teacher education candidate can use the charts and tables in this chapter for assignments in your professional education courses. Your peers and professors will be asking you for directions to create this material. If the alternative certification candidate is currently teaching, he or she can create and use this material in the classroom. If the candidate is taking teacher education courses, this information will also be useful for class projects and assignments.

This chapter focuses on a variety of teaching strategies to help students learn. Today's classrooms are far from homogeneous in nature; therefore, a potpourri of strategies will be presented with a heterogeneous group or multiple levels of learners in mind.

As you read about the various teaching strategies in this chapter, keep in mind that they are both an ends to a mean and a means to an end. They involve both the learning and the assessment. As a classroom teacher, consider using a single sheet of paper per student for an entire week of class work, as opposed to running off one ditto worksheet per student per day. For example, a detailed KWL chart provides you with recorded information throughout the week's lessons (the equivalent of five worksheets) and can also be used as an assessment of the content of the week's lessons. Rather than laboring over the photocopying machine to duplicate five sets of worksheets per child for the week, you can provide each student with a single sheet of paper. The K and W portions of the chart could be daily grades, and the L section could be recorded as a test grade. The same concept of student work time and assessment can be used with each of the teaching strategies discussed in this chapter.

As you read the following pages, think outside the lines or outside the box. View these strategies through the eyes of a seasoned professional who would utilize them to promote learning and still provide an assessment of the objectives and concepts.

The teaching strategies presented in this chapter can be connected to the major learning theories. You will learn strategies that are advocated by the educational researchers in the next chapter—David Ausubel, Jerome Bruner, Lev Vygotsky, Jean Piaget, and Howard Gardner. The strategies not only are theory based but also appeal to the various learning modalities.

KWL CHART/KWHL CHART

The KWL chart can be used with any age or learning level but is most frequently used at the elementary level at the present time. KWL learning can also be used with virtually any curricular area. The charts can be a class project, or they can be used with older students who have the writing ability to complete their personal charts themselves. KWL charts can be on a chalkboard or become an interactive bulletin board. These charts can be designed for individual student use and photocopied on a standard sized sheet of paper. This teaching strategy is flexible in design and can be used with a wide variety of

learners. The many variations on this approach are limited only by your imagination (Grant and Vansledright 2001: 70).

The true beauty of KWL charts is that they appeal to the auditory, visual,
and kinesthetic learners. When KWL charts are presented as a class project or
as a group activity, they appeal to the auditory and visual learners. When they
are presented as an individual project, the student must write (kinesthetic),
view the completed project (visual), and explain their chart to the class as well
as hear the explanations of others (auditory). In my university methods
courses, I refer to this as "hitting a home run" or "batting a thousand" because
you have covered all three learning modalities.

KWL learning can be broken down into three phases: (1) What do we
know? (2) What do we *want* to know? (3) What did we *learn?* KWL learning can also be broken into a two-phase process by combining parts 1 and
2 together at the beginning and using 3 as a conclusion, summation, and
assessment.

Table 2.1. KWL Chart

Student's name _____ Date started _____ Date completed _____		
Topic:		
What do I KNOW?	What do I WANT to know?	What did I LEARN?

⚓ **Technology Excursion Trip**   *This KWL chart was created by opening Word,
going to Table, then Insert. I used Two Rows, One Column. I adjusted the height of
my rows to fit the content I wished to use. I then went back and highlighted the bottom row, returned to Table, Split Cells. I split the bottom row into three cells of
equal size.*

   For the KWLH chart, you would split the cells into four cells of equal size.

Table 2.2. Seahorse KWL Chart

| Student's name _Susan Jones_ Date started _____ Date completed _____ | | |
| Topic: _Seahorses_ | | |
What do I KNOW?	What do I WANT to know?	What did I LEARN?
Live in the ocean _Look like a horse_	_What or how do they eat?_ _How big are they?_ _How do they swim or stay still?_	• _Suck micro-organisms through their mouth_ • _Range in size from an inch to several inches in length_ • _Curl their tails around seaweed to stay in place_ • _The male gives birth_ • _Seahorses can change color_ • _Each eye can move in different directions_

Table 2.1 is a sample of a KWL chart that you can create using a word processor. This sample can be used as a class, group, or individual project. Table 2.2 is a KWL chart that has completed all three phases.

A similar version of the KWL chart is the KWHL chart. This chart is virtually the same but has the addition of the "How are we going to find out?" phase. The answer to this question would vary from problem to problem depending

Table 2.3. KWHL Chart

| Student's name _____ Date started _____ Date completed _____ | | | |
| Topic: | | | |
What do I KNOW?	What do I WANT to know?	HOW are we going to find out?	What did I LEARN?

on the question, but it might include such responses as "Conduct an Internet search," "Use an encyclopedia," "Check an atlas," or "Use a dictionary." Table 2.3 is an example of a blank KWHL chart.

The contents of the KWL or KWHL charts can become a springboard for a variety of writing activities, such as maintaining a journal over the span of the project or creating an assessment or evaluation.

References

Ogle, D. 1986. K-W-L: A teaching model that develops active reading of expository text. *Reading Teacher* 39: 564–70.

Grant, S. G., and B. Vansledright. 2001. *Constructing a powerful approach to teaching and learning in elementary social studies.* Boston: Houghton Mifflin.

Web References

http://teachers.teach-nology.com

www.abcteach.com

www.ecesc.k12.in.us

www.silosandsmokestacks.org/resources/FieldTripGuide/the_kwl_chart.htm

www.nscu.edu/midlink/KWL.chart.html. Offers samples of charts

www.graphic.org/kwhl.html. Adds the *H* to the traditional KWL chart, for "How are we going to find out?" and shows a sample of a KWHL chart.

CONCEPT MAPPING OR CONCEPT WEBBING

Some textbooks refer to the next teaching strategy as *concept mapping*; others use the term *concept webbing*. Like Blackjack and Twenty-One, they are basically the same. Within the context of this section, the terms are intended to be synonymous.

Concept mapping or concept webbing can be used with any age group of students working with any curricular area. If the students do not have the writing skills to complete the map or web by themselves, the task can become a class project, with the teacher recording the students' verbal responses. Students who have developed writing skills at an independent level can work with this concept as a group or individual assignment.

Concept mapping or concept webbing is an example of visual, graphic, or iconic representation of concepts with bridges showing relationships. Students organize their thoughts in written form. The general procedure is to have students (1) identify important concepts in materials being studied; (2) rank-order or prioritize the concepts from the most general to the most specific; and then (3) arrange the concepts on a sheet of paper, connect related ideas with lines, and define the connections between the related ideas. Concept mapping or webbing gives students the opportunity to classify, prioritize, organize, and record their thoughts. This teaching strategy also follows David Ausubel's theory of meaningful verbal learning—building a bridge to connect new knowledge to previously learned knowledge or past experiences.

I used concept maps with my elementary students for many years. At the fifth grade level, the students worked independently on their maps. The learning process met the learning modality needs of the auditory, visual, and kinesthetic learner. In the VARK study, even the reading/writing learning modality was met.

As a fifth grade teacher, I used concept maps as a teaching strategy throughout the years with my science and social studies students. All students at the fifth grade level were required to take a state criterion-referenced writing test. Teachers administering the tests were required to collect any used papers following the exams. When I collected the used papers, I could see that most of the students had chosen to organize their thoughts by using a concept map rather than the age-old and much-disliked outline form. Their knowledge base for using concept maps in science and social studies had been transferred to another curricular area.

Concept mapping or webbing has also been included in all the elementary methods courses I have taught. Adult learners get out their paper and pencils and construct maps just as elementary or secondary students would. The university methods textbooks connect concept mapping with Ausubel and also the writings of Lev Vygotsky.

When first introducing concept maps to your students, you might want to provide them with examples or with a map in which they only need to complete the blanks. Figure 2.1 shows an example of a blank concept map that could be used to introduce students to this topic.

After a few exercises in this manner, the students will be able to design and complete the maps independently. Each one will be unique. Provide an opportunity to use the chalkboard or whiteboard or use an overhead transparency to display and discuss their work. Figure 2.2 shows a standard concept map or concept web.

FIGURE 2.1
Concept map template

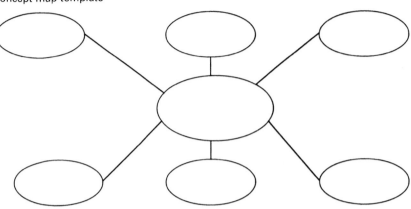

FIGURE 2.2
Concept map: animal adaptations in winter

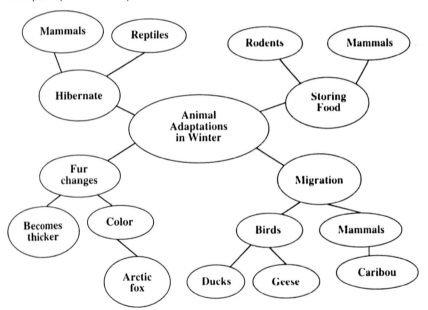

✝ **Technology Excursion Trip** *A concept map template can be made by using AutoShapes in Word. Create a Word document, go to Insert, Picture, then AutoShapes, and decide which shape you want to use for your concept map. The example here uses ovals throughout the map. You can select a different shape for each level as well as a different color for each level. To create the connecting lines, I used AutoShapes again and selected Line. This allowed me to begin and end my line wherever I chose.*

Figure 2.3
Concept map: using a variety of shapes

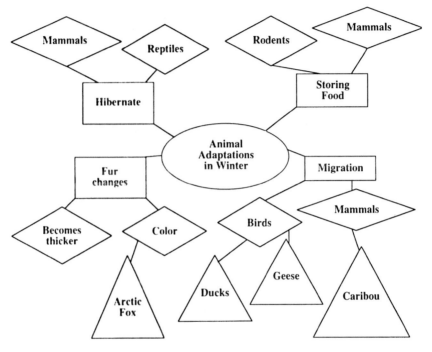

Teachers can assist students with learning problems by introducing differ-ent shapes or the use of colors. For example, the core concept in the center can be a different shape or a different color. The first level of priority might be an-other shape or color. The second level of priority might be displayed by a dif-ferent shape and another color. Figure 2.3 shows a concept map with varying shapes to show the different levels of priority.

Concept maps can be used to answer the questions Who? What? Where? When? Why? and How many? or How much? Figure 2.4 depicts a concept map used to answer some of these questions about the topic of the western movement in the United States. This map could be modified to use various color codes or shapes to assist with learning also.

References

Kellough, R. D. 1996. *Integrating mathematics and science for intermediate and middle school students.* Englewood Cliffs, N.J.: Merrill/Prentice Hall.

FIGURE 2.4
Concept map: who? what? when? where? how?

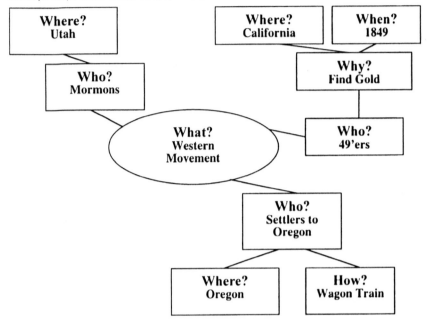

Maxim, G. W. 1999. *Social studies and the elementary school child.* 6th ed. Upper
Saddle River, N.J.: Merrill/Prentice Hall.

Wolfinger, D. M. 2000. *Science in the elementary and middle school.* New York:
Addison Wesley Longman.

COOPERATIVE LEARNING

Cooperative learning, or collaborative learning, is a heterogeneous group
learning environment in which every member of the group has an active role.
There is no single magic number of group members; however, experts suggest
groups consisting of four or five students is best. As the teacher, you can
choose the number of group members that best meets the needs of your
learning activity or best utilizes the number of students in your class.

Rather than taking a competitive approach to learning, cooperative learning instills exactly what it intends—the cooperation of each member of the
group to achieve learning. Cooperative learning promotes the old motto of

the Three Musketeers: "All for one and one for all." Every individual in the group is a vital component in successfully completing the project. Each member of the group cooperates or collaborates, as opposed to competes, to achieve the end result. Cooperative learning strategies provide small-group interaction for all types of learners, all levels of learners, and students with a spectrum of language abilities. Therefore, cooperative learning strategies benefit special needs students and ESL/LEP students well as the average child and the academically gifted student. It provides a win/win learning environment in which every member is valued and important.

There are three major components when initiating a cooperative learning activity with your class. The first phase is *planning*, or determining the objectives for the lesson and the number of students per group that can attain those objectives. As the classroom teacher, take a proactive approach to group selection rather than allowing students to select their own groups. Establish a small set of rules of order to be utilized by the groups. These rules can vary from your general classroom rules. The teacher may establish the rules prior to the group activity, or the class can establish rules as a class consensus. Examples might include "The group members only speak with each other," "Remain seated until the time frame is completed," or "Lower your voice when working with your group." Order can soon turn to chaos without establishing any guidelines prior to group activities.

The second phase is *implementation*, or conducting the activity with the students. Designate group members, go over the activity rules, assign the parameters of the project, discuss the various ways in which the goals can be attained, give a time frame for the project, and explain the evaluation system.

The final phase is *evaluation* or *assessment*. Will you provide an evaluation instrument the group completes together? Will you evaluate every member individually? Will the students evaluate each member of the group in a "peer evaluation"? Will the instrument be in a "supply" form in which the students supply the answers? Will the instrument be in a "select" form in which the students select the correct answer from several choices? Will the instrument be a combination of both supply and select?

The jigsaw model is a cooperative learning technique developed by Elliot Aronson and colleagues (1978) that is a combination of cooperative and individual learning. Just as a jigsaw puzzle is small pieces that when put together form a completed whole, the jigsaw approach to cooperative learning allows each member to be responsible for one portion. The members of the group working together form the whole completed project.

Slavin (1986) modified Aronson's jigsaw model, calling it Jigsaw II. Rather than working on a part of the whole, students working with the Jigsaw II model take part in a common learning experience. They learn all parts together.

Web References

www.ed.gov/databases/ERIC_Digests/ed370991.html. Describes the essential elements of cooperative learning in the classroom.

http://712educ.../blhelpclinfo.htm?iam=dpile&terms=%2Bcoopera-tive+%2Bgroup+2%Blearnin. Includes information on cooperative learning and benefits.

www.cde.ca.gov/iasa/cooplrng2.html. The site for the article "Cooperative Learning Response to Diversity."

MNEMONICS

Professionals generally avoid the use of rote memorization in daily learning activities. There are times, however, when rote memorization is necessary. An example of rote memorization is learning your social security number or your address. "Learning by rote is easier if one can connect that which is to be memorized to some prior knowledge. Often used to bridge the gap between rote learning and meaningful learning is the strategy known as *mnemonics*, which is any strategy that will assist memory" (Kellough 1996: 20).

Some examples of mnemonics include the following:

- The nine planets in our solar system in order from the sun can be learned in a sentence such as My very educated mother just served us nine pizzas (Mercury, Venus, Earth, Mars, Jupiter, Saturn, Uranus, Neptune, and Pluto).
- The colors of the spectrum in order can be learned by an individual's name: ROY G BIV, which stands for Red, Orange, Yellow, Green, Blue, Indigo, and Violet.
- Learning the names of the lines and spaces of the upper staff or treble clef is difficult for children. The age-old mnemonic aid for the spaces is FACE, which literally gives the name of each space. The accepted mnemonic aid for the lines is Every good boy does fine, which stand for EGBDF.

• When learning the three primary colors in art class, consider Read your book to stand for red, yellow, and blue. When learning the three secondary colors in art class, consider very good opera to stand for violet, green, and orange.

Mnemonics can be presented to students in either a horizontal or vertical form. Some students will actually prefer the vertical form. Use either presentation, along with various colors, to help students learn and also retain knowledge. The following is an example of the primary colors rearranged in a vertical form:

Read

Your

Book

Mnemonics can be utilized in any curricular area. I have used this concept with elementary students at various grade levels as well as with adult learners in my methods courses in art, social studies, science, and language arts. In public school art, students were required to know the elements of art and also the principles of art. Each area had approximately seven concepts to remember. The students wrote their own personal mnemonics system to assist them prior to the tests. Mnemonics could be presented as a class project or a group project as well as an individual task. Obviously, my teacher education candidates had high levels of writing abilities and could complete this task independently. Students with language or writing limitations could use mnemonics as a class project with the teacher as the recorder. Students with more developed writing skills could use mnemonics as a group or individual project.

If you are beginning a mnemonics activity with your students, consider completing this as a class project the first time or first few times. Allow the students to become comfortable with the process. If your students have the ability to write independently, you can then move on to small groups working together. Depending on the writing abilities of your students, after the students are capable of working in small groups, allow them to complete mnemonics tasks independently and share their ideas with the class.

One fun "ice breaker" idea to introduce mnemonics is to ask the students to design a mnemonic phrase from the letters of their first name. Establish a rule that it must be the entire first name or a nickname, such as Jenny for Jennifer or Bob for Robert. Another question to address is the order of the letters. They can all come in order *or* be arranged out of order. Let the students know in advance. Here is a mnemonic phrase based on *Linda*:

Lively

Individual's

Never

Daunting

Attitude

A mnemonic phrase for *Jonah* is the following:

Jonah

Only

Needs

A

Horse

Reference
Kellough, R. D. 1996. *Integrating mathematics and science for intermediate and middle school students.* Englewood Cliffs, N.J.: Merrill/Prentice Hall.

Web Reference
A variety of mnemonics can be found on the web. Go to a large search engine, such as www.AltaVista.com, www.google.com, or www.dogpile.com. Type in *mnemonics.* This activity can also be completed by students of an appropriate age as either an individual or group assignment.

EVENT CHAINS OR TIME LINES
Event chains and time lines are still another form of graphic or iconic representation. Students must organize or sequence the events in order from first through last. Event chains or time lines represent all the parts of a whole

through iconic or visual representation. An example of a topic to use with an event chain or a time line could be the Civil War. Students would begin with the firing on Fort Sumter, the major events and battles during the war, and the date of the signing of the treaty at the Appomattox Courthouse.

Time lines can be easily created using cash register tape. Borrow a roll from the office rather than purchasing one yourself. Your students will only use a small fraction of the roll. After the students have designed their time lines sequentially on their regular notebook paper, give them a piece of cash register tape and ask them to create a time line that runs horizontally. They can write in the important dates and events. Time lines can be highly detailed or very simple in nature. The completed project will be a graphic representation in sequential order.

Time lines can also be created by using plain photocopy paper. After the students have written down important facts on the notebook paper, this information can be transferred to create a time line on a plain sheet of paper. The student will need a ruler or straight edge to draw the lines for the time line. Figure 2.5 is a basic template for a time line.

An event chain is much like a time line, except it runs vertically rather than horizontally. The level of complexity varies greatly. You can design a blank

FIGURE 2.5
Student time line template

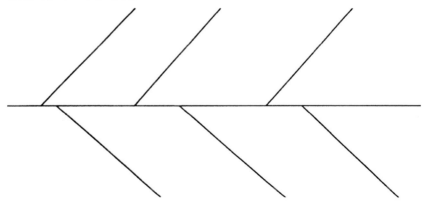

⚓ **Technology Excursion Trip**   *This template was created by opening Word, and selecting AutoShapes. The lines were created by using the symbol that creates lines and looks like "\". When you put the cursor over that shape, the word line will appear. Simply select that symbol and then go to the space on the page where you wish to begin your line. When you left-click on the mouse, the line will stop. You must return to the toolbar to select the line once again to continue this process.*

FIGURE 2.6
Event chain template

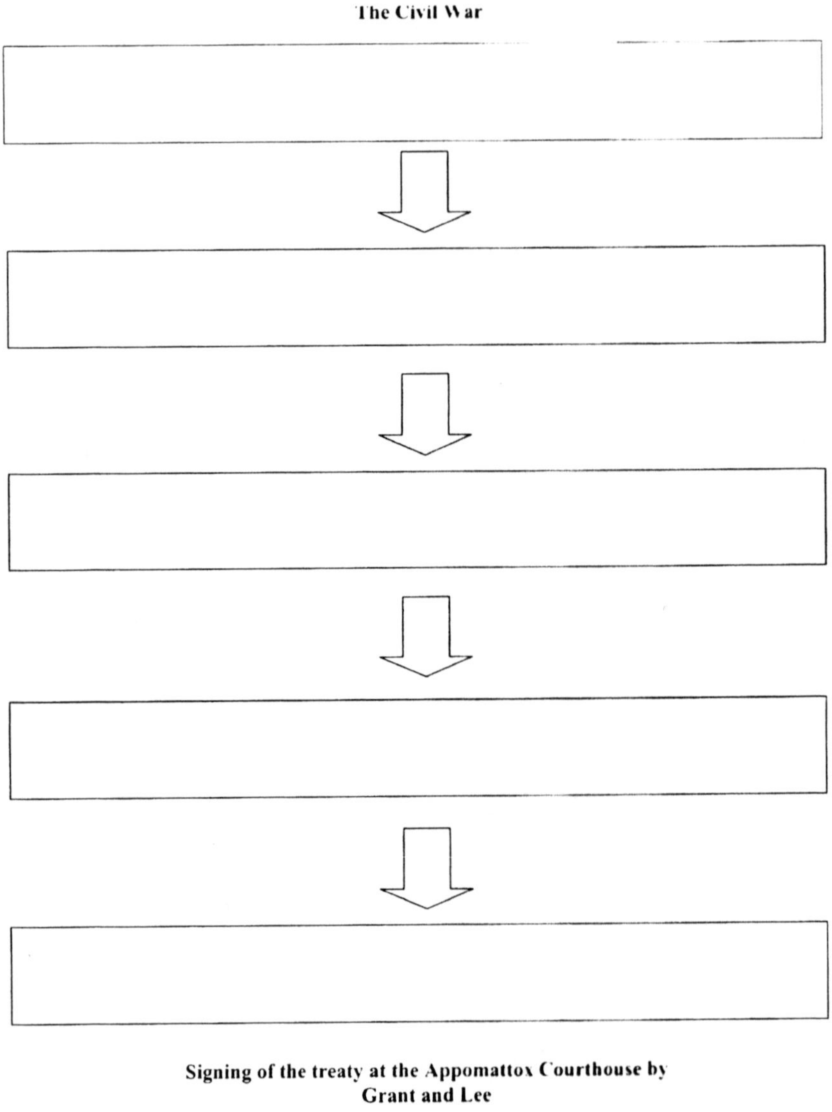

The Civil War

**Signing of the treaty at the Appomattox Courthouse by
Grant and Lee**

✦ **Technology Excursion Trip**   *This event chain was created by opening Word, Insert,
and selecting Text Box. You can make the boxes any size you wish. To create the arrows
between each box, use AutoShapes, Block Arrows. You can choose from several arrows.*

chain for the students to write their answers in the blanks (see figure 2.6). After the students have had experience creating event chains, they can design their own and will not need to rely on a blank form.

CHAINS

A tactile activity for students that is similar to event chains or time lines is a simple chain. Chains can be used in reading class to reconstruct the major events of the story—sequencing. Chains can be created in language arts or foreign language classes to show the progression of the verb tenses or the verb and pronoun association. Language arts students could actually create a chain with the number of links corresponding to the number of words in the sentence. Each word could be written on a link along with the part of speech for that word. The writing or links could be color coded for special services students—a noun link would be red, a verb link would be blue, adjectives would be yellow, and so forth. The color-coding system would also be good for primary students who are just learning the parts of speech.

I used chains to physically show students the food chain. Younger students have difficulty mentally constructing the progression of the food chain of a specific biome or habitat. If you give them a slip of paper—the link that will be added to the food chain—they can then work with a group to design a food chain.

My favorite way to introduce the food chain concept is to brainstorm with the class about the mascots of professional football teams. We then take the animal mascots and divide the students into smaller groups to construct a food chain. Each student writes the name of one mascot onto their link, and the links are assembled with a glue stick or staple. There are times when two different chains must be constructed—one for the carnivores and one for the herbivores. The use of color-coded links will help students with learning problems see the difference between a carnivore chain with one color and a herbivore chain with another color. Older students can be responsible for finding the genus and species of the animals and writing these on the link along with the animal's name. This same concept could be done with the mascots of college or professional baseball, hockey, or basketball teams.

Event chains constructed on paper (previously mentioned) can be transposed to a true chain using slips of paper to represent the links. The event chain of the Civil War could be easily changed to a chain by giving the students slips of paper and a glue stick.

Chains can be an individual student activity or a group activity. As the teacher you design the specifications of the lesson—one chain per group or one chain per group member. You will also have the opportunity to set up the criteria and the point value for assessment of a chain learning activity.

Chains appeal to visual, kinesthetic, and auditory learners. The addition of color-coded links will benefit students with learning problems and also enhance learning for visual learners. When the students verbally explain their chains, this activity is connected to Ausubel's meaningful verbal learning theory. Chains also appeal to Bruner's enactive learning and iconic representation. Chains created in a cooperative group setting tie to the theory and writings of Vygotsky.

CYCLES

Another example of iconic or graphic representation is the cycle. Cycles occur in time, such as the days of the week, the months, and the seasons. Cycles occur in science in the stages of life, such as the metamorphosis of a frog or butterfly. Another cyclical science phenomenon is the water cycle.

The level of cycles varies in complexity, just as it does with the event chain. If you are teaching very young students, they can draw the cycle rather than writing out the explanation. You can design a blank cycle form for the students to complete or they can complete their own from scratch. Figure 2.7 is a sample of the life cycle of a butterfly.

VENN DIAGRAMS

John Venn first introduced Venn diagrams in England in 1880. These diagrams consist of two or more overlapping circles. The overlapping area is used to show relationships. Venn diagrams can be used with any age group, in any curricular area, to provide the students with visual or iconic representation of relationships between or among two or more sets. Students can utilize the visual, kinesthetic, and auditory learning modalities by creating their own Venn diagrams and sharing their results with the class. Venn diagrams

FIGURE 2.7
Cycle

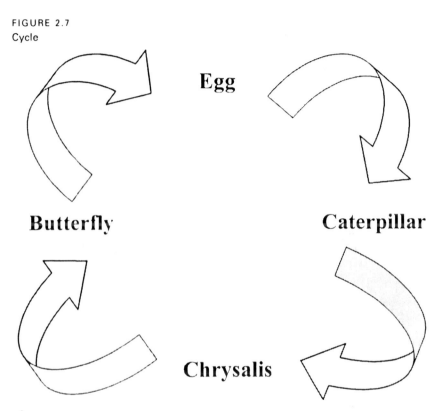

Egg

Butterfly

Caterpillar

Chrysalis

🏃 **Technology Excursion Trip** *The cycle was created by opening Word, Insert, and making a selection from AutoShapes. Block Arrows offers a curved arrow choice that I used. It gives the illusion of movement from one stage to the next.*

can be used in a cooperative group activity, as an individual assignment, or as a class project.

Figure 2.8 shows two overlapping circles as a Venn diagram. Note the mutual information in the overlapping section. Figure 2.9 shows three overlapping circles as a Venn diagram.

One variation of Venn diagrams is the use of colors to help students with learning problems grasp the concepts. The colors variations can be used with the writing within the circles, in the background spaces of the circles, or in the actual outlines of the circles. Color variations also appeal to visual learners.

In mathematics, Venn diagrams are used to show the relationship between sets. In language arts, Venn diagrams are used to show similarities and

FIGURE 2.8
Venn diagram: shark and whale

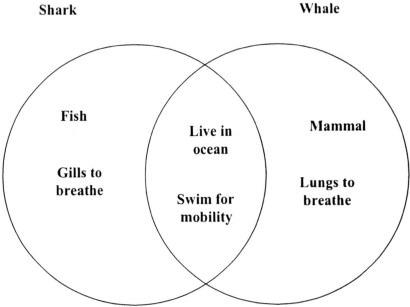

differences in characters, stories, poems, and so forth. They also can be used in science or social studies to show similarities and differences or divide further to show genus or habitat.

Venn diagrams can become a kinesthetic learning activity by having the students "construct" the circles and manipulate them. Inexpensive paper plates can be used for this activity. Every student or group will receive two paper plates. Ask them to cut along the center ridge inside the plate. The end result will produce the ribbed or ridged portion intact with a large hole in the center. Use a hole punch to punch one hole in the ridge portion of each plate. Put the plates together, lining up the holes, and hold together using a brad. The students can manipulate the plates to vary the width of the overlapping area. By placing a sheet of paper *under* the paper plate manipulative, the students have a place to write their responses. Once the manipulatives have been constructed, they can be stored and used throughout the school year. This is a very inexpensive way to provide learning opportunities that utilize the learning theories of Ausubel, Bruner, Vygotsky, and Gardner.

FIGURE 2.9
Venn diagram template for three items

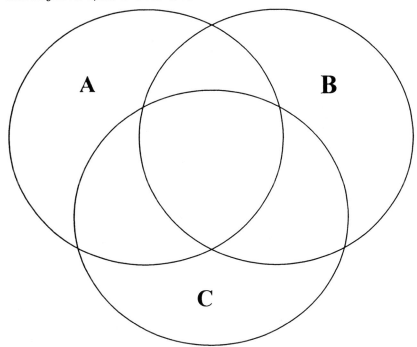

Technology Excursion Trip   *The teacher or older students can create the circles for an easy-to-create template using the computer. Open Word; go to Insert, Picture, AutoShapes. Select a circle or oval. Play with the size until you have the size you desire. With the "boxes" around the shape, go to Edit, Copy. You will now Paste this shape onto the page. Adjust the shape so that it overlaps the present circle or oval you have.*

Now right-click on Format AutoShapes. Left-click under the topic of No Fill under the Fill (color) category at the top. Then select OK. This will make the circle continue its shape.

To make three or more circles for your Venn diagram, continue step 2 as many times as you wish.

To create text within your Venn diagram, follow these steps:

1. *Go to Insert, Text Box. Place the text box in the desired location. Type the text in the box*
2. *With the "boxes" selected, go to Format—Text Box. Left-click on Line—Color—No Line—OK. Your lines for the Text Box will erase.*

A second way to use Venn diagrams with children is with the visual aid of hula hoops. These colorful and inexpensive children's toys can also form the circles of a Venn diagram. The hoops can rest on the tray of a whiteboard or chalkboard. The teacher or students can add text using chalk or markers to create the Venn diagram.

A third way to use this teaching strategy is with a single sheet of paper on which the students create their own Venn diagrams (see figure 2.10). The students can write their text in the lines below the diagram in the proper spaces.

Create a template to compare and contrast two things by following the example in figure 2.10. The Venn diagram is at the top of the page. Lines have been drawn to divide the remainder of the page into thirds to allow the students specific space to write down their information.

A variation of this Venn diagram would be to fold the standard 8.5 × 11-inch paper horizontally (a "hamburger bun" fold as opposed to a "hot dog bun" fold that would be vertical—lengthwise). On the top of the paper, draw the Venn diagram. Then make three cuts through the Venn diagram—to allow three spaces to show the characteristics of each group as well as the similarities. You now have flaps in which the students can lift up and write the information *under* each flap. Figure 2.11 shows the flaps raised to show the students' writing.

The Venn diagrams created by John Venn over one hundred years ago have been modified slightly over the years. Today they do not have to be created using "circles." Silhouettes or profile outlines can be used to compare and contrast two sets, represented by images. This new wave of Venn diagrams opens up the concept of visual literacy to a new realm.

First grade teacher Maria Walther uses the overlapping outline profiles of presidents George Washington and Abraham Lincoln as the basis of her Venn diagram, which is presented on a bulletin board. "Her students volunteer unique qualities about each man as well as qualities they shared. The shared qualities are inserted where Washington and Lincoln's heads overlap; unique qualities are placed on the faces of the respective presidents" (Farris 2001: 21). Silhouettes of the profiles of Washington and Lincoln are just one set of examples of shapes that can be used for Venn diagrams. Various shapes can be used to show the relationship between and among groups.

FIGURE 2.10
Students list information below Venn diagram

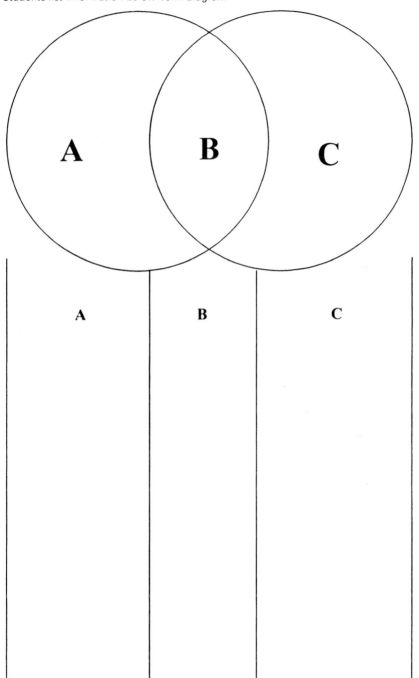

FIGURE 2.11
Student writes in answers to create flaps

	Fold	
WHALES	**ALIKE or SIMILAR**	**SHARKS**
Mammals	Live in ocean	Fish
Skeleton made of bones	Swim for mobility	Skeleton made of cartilage
Breathe through lungs	Toothed whales and sharks have large teeth and eat other fish and mammals	Breathe through gills
Tail fin moves up and down		Tail fin moves side to side

CUT   CUT

Reference

Farris, Pamela J. 2002. *Teaching the language arts: Process, product, and assessment.* 3d ed. Boston: McGraw-Hill, 19–21.

Web References

www.sdcoe.k12.ca.us/score/actbank/tvenn.htm. Provides some information regarding Venn diagrams and one example.

www.venndiagram.com/toptenvenn.html. Describes ten ways to use Venn diagrams.

www.sue.csc.uvic.ca/~cos.venn. Features several links for visuals and information regarding Venn diagrams.

CONCLUSION

This chapter has offered a variety of teaching strategies for you to implement in your teaching repertoire. Bruner would refer to these as offering opportunities as both *enactive* learning and utilizing *iconic* representation.

A quotation used frequently in teacher education circles is "What is taught is not necessarily what is learned." Educators work every day to teach strategically planned objectives to students. The students do not necessarily learn the objective. This chapter gives the teacher a "plan B"—an alternative strategy to use tomorrow to teach the same objective, and, hopefully, the student will learn it then.

Connecting Strategies to Educational Theories

This chapter is designed for all three groups of readers. Whether you are a teacher education candidate preparing to enter the classroom after graduation, a seasoned and practicing teacher, or an individual who has become a teacher through alternative certification, the contents of this chapter will appeal to you. A very brief overview of the various theories is presented, describing the works of Jean Piaget, David Ausubel, Jerome Bruner, Lev Vygotsky, and Howard Gardner.

JEAN PIAGET

No chapter on student acquisition of knowledge could be complete without a brief discussion of the writings of Jean Piaget, the Swiss zoologist, philosopher, and epistemologist. He became interested in child development after he meticulously took notes on the mental growth and development of his own children. Piaget's stages of cognitive development—sensorimotor, preoperational, concrete operational, and formal operational—are taught in virtually all educational psychology courses across the country. Table 3.1 describes the four developmental stages.

Egocentric students see the world through their own eyes. They have not attained a level to take another person's point of view. Through life experiences with others, they move out of this phase.

Conservation, according to Wolfinger (2000), is the ability to realize that a change in the appearance of an object does not change the quantity of that object. Preoperational students have difficulty seeing quantities as changing.

Table 3.1.   Piaget's Stages of Development

Sensorimotor: Birth–18 months	Preoperational: 18 months–6.5 years	Concrete Operational: 6.5–11 or 12 years	Formal Operational: 11 or 12 years to adult
• Children think through actions	• Language develops • Communication skills • Egocentric	• Conservation of numbers, substance, length, area, weight, and time • Verbal reasoning • Concepts of conservation and reversibility	• Hypothesizing • Students learn by reading, listening, and concrete experiences

They are thus considered "nonconservers." Conservation is attained in the concrete operational stage.

Reversibility is the ability to work forward and backward in your thought process. An example of reversibility in mathematics is "6 + 4 = 10, 10 − 6 = 4." Subtraction is the reverse operation of addition, just as division is the reverse operation of multiplication. Students in science learn the three forms of matter—solid, liquid, and gas. Reversibility thinkers know that liquids will freeze and then reverse to liquid when warmed.

Although most texts suggest that the formal operational stage begins at age eleven or twelve, Wolfinger suggests that this is more likely to occur at age fifteen or later. "This may be considered to begin with the development of conservation of volume and extend throughout adulthood" (Wolfinger 2000: 42).

Three areas of Piaget's writings that will be reviewed in this chapter are the concepts of *schema, assimilation,* and *accommodation.* (*Schema* is the singular form; *schemata* is the plural form.) *Schema* is generally referred to as a "mental file folder" into which one puts knowledge. The "file folder" is used to identify, process, organize, and store incoming information. Individuals can classify specific experiences and information through this "filing system."

Piaget borrowed the term *assimilation* from biology, "where it refers to the process by which an organism eats food, digests it, and then assimilates or changes it into a usable form" (Heinich et al. 2002: 7). Assimilation of schema occurs when one's existing cognitive structure requires little modification to include the new idea. "With new experiences, the schema expands in size but does not change its basic structure. Using the process of assimilation, the individual attempts to place new concepts into existing schemata" (Heinich et al. 2002: 7).

If, however, no relevant schemata exist, new behavior sequences are built up through experimentation, instruction, or both. The process of either modifying existing schemata or creating ones is what Piaget refers to as *accommodation*. You have heard the expression that one cannot fit a square peg into a round hole. This expression ties back to accommodation. When the square peg does not fit, there are two possible responses by the learner, according to Heinich et al. (2002): (1) The learner can create a new schema into which the new stimulus is placed, or (2) the existing schema can be modified so that the new stimulus will fit—the modification of the square peg *or* the modification of the round hole. Both cases are processes of accommodation.

My best example of the concepts of schema, assimilation, and accommodation comes from a life experience of my nephew, Joel. When he was a preschooler, Joel labored over maps and the family globe to design the family vacation—a trip to China. His father was a social studies teacher; thus, Joel had an idea of the representations of maps and the globe. He knew where we were (the United States), and he knew where the Great Wall of China was located. He decided that the family would pack up the station wagon and head off for China—a road trip. When he presented his vacation plans to his family, Joel discovered a vital element that greatly disrupted his plans. He learned that the blue section on maps and the globe represented the oceans. Because he could touch it and see it, he thought the blue part was just like the green part.

Translating this story into Piaget's terms, Joel had a set plan for the family vacation in his mental file folder system—his schema. Joel had his mental file folder, he assimilated his knowledge into that file folder, but he had to use the accommodation process to determine that his family would not be able to drive from Oklahoma to China.

This story is a cute tale about a three-year-old; however, adults utilize the processes of assimilation and accommodation throughout each day as well. Sometimes we make mistakes in our processes and must reassimilate and reaccommodate our data. I remember my father's story about the very first time he saw a jet airplane streak across the sky. He was convinced that it was a spaceship filled with aliens. He was in the country fishing with a friend at a farm pond. They decided to return to town and tell no one about the mysterious thing they had seen in the sky. Later that day, the radio (because they didn't have televisions then) reported that the first jet plane had flown over the Tulsa, Oklahoma, area. Fortunately the conclusion they jumped to was incorrect. Through going through the process of assimilation and accommodation a second time, my father now had a new mental file folder marked "jet airplane."

Piaget's concepts of schema, assimilation, and accommodation are the cornerstones of student learning. Throughout this chapter and throughout the book you will be reminded to connect the content of the lesson to previously learned knowledge—we build a bridge from the student's knowledge to new information. This is the way we all learn. Students need visual, verbal, and manipulative or kinesthetic cues to assist them in making these connections.

The best tip that I give my elementary methods students is to connect to previously learned knowledge in the *introduction* portion of the lesson. Just one or two sentences can set the stage for learning. Begin with the phrase "As you recall, yesterday we learned about . . . Today we are going to . . ." By connecting yesterday's concept to that of today's, the students are immediately assimilating content of the lesson. Those file folders are already busy! For example, "As you recall, yesterday we learned how to find the perimeter of a square. Today we are going to use a similar formula to find the perimeter of a rectangle." The teacher is building a bridge from the student's previously learned knowledge base to concepts to be learned today. Use this tip in *every* lesson *every* day. Your students will benefit from your endeavors.

As an elementary teacher, I sometimes taught as many as thirteen different lessons each day (remember that I had multiple reading and mathematics groups). Not only did the children have trouble remembering what we did yesterday, but so did I. It was a habit—or crutch—that I developed to help all of us. Sometimes I would verbally connect our lesson to what was studied yesterday. Other times I would ask a student to tell the class about the content of the previous lesson. Either way was a "win-win" situation for everyone.

In one situation my student teacher became my colleague, working just down the hall from me. I often would pass her opened door and hear that magic phrase as she introduced a lesson. (In her case, it was with a strong Long Island, New York, accent rather than my traditional Oklahoma twang, but I still relished hearing it.)

As a university representative supervising student teachers and first-year teachers, I *always* hear this phrase when I visit the classroom of one of my former students. Make this practice a part of your daily repertoire. Your colleagues and administrator will notice. Most important, your students will benefit from this practice, which connects to the writings of Piaget.

One final suggestion: In concluding or closing the lesson, review what was covered today and connect the contents with *tomorrow's* lesson or *next week's* topic. Give the students a *review* and also a *preview*. It will take less than one minute of instruction time, but your students will benefit greatly. Rather than viewing learning as a daily grind of fragmented learning, they will begin to make connections and see the whole picture. And they will go home and tell their parents or caregivers. This will also show evidence of your planning abilities. You must have lessons and units well planned in advance to be able to tell the students about future learning opportunities.

DAVID AUSUBEL—MEANINGFUL VERBAL LEARNING

David Ausubel is associated with the theory of meaningful verbal learning. He urged teachers to use learning situations and examples that are familiar to the children, which helps children assimilate what is being learned with what they already know, making their learning more meaningful. Ausubel also encouraged teachers to "make the learning meaningful and longer lasting by using advance organizers, ideas that are presented to students before the new material and that mentally prepare them to integrate the new material into previously built cognitive structures" (Roberts 1996: 16). As a teacher, you are building a bridge to connect previously learned knowledge with the new information of the lesson. You are striving to make learning "meaningful," according to Ausubel. The teaching strategies using KWL charts, KWHL charts, concept maps, event chains, time lines, chains, cycles, and Venn diagrams provide visual or graphic organizers for students to both learn and also retain knowledge.

JEROME BRUNER—DISCOVERY LEARNING

Jerome Bruner is associated with discovery learning. Bruner believed that learners acquire knowledge in one of three phases, ranging from the very concrete to the abstract. Bruner refers to these phases as the three modes of know-

Table 3.2.   Modes of Learning

Symbolic Mode	Iconic Mode	Enactive Mode
Charts, tables, graphs, newspapers, maps, written and oral language	Pictures, videos, CDs, replicas, simulations, models	Experiments, field trips, guest speakers, real items/artifacts, class activities, manipulatives

Source: Adapted from Maxim (1999).

ing (see table 3.2). An example of "concrete" is something familiar and tangible such as a fish or spoon. An example of "abstract" is the concept of freedom or hope.

Bruner's *enactive* learning involved concrete hands-on activities. *Iconic* learning is based on the use of visual imagery using representations of real objects when the objects themselves cannot be directly experienced. Iconic imagery includes pictures, videos, CDs, replicas, simulations, and models. Bruner believed that *iconic* representation meant representing reality through imagery. Bruner's final learning phase, *symbolic representation*, is the most abstract. Symbolic representation, through written and oral language, enables students to think abstractly beyond mere experience and pictures. Examples of symbolic representation include charts, tables, graphs, newspapers, and maps. It allows them to conceptualize through processes of reflective thought (Ellis 1998: 54). Other major theorists, most teachers, school districts, local boards of education, and state departments of education focus on the question "*What* is learned?" This information is attained by testing and assessment. Bruner looks instead at "*How* is it learned?" By incorporating the concepts of the learning modalities and the teaching strategies from the previous chapter, teachers can recognize the element of how a student learns.

The teaching strategies discussed and illustrated in the previous chapter that connect to Bruner's iconic or graphic learning are KWL charts, KWHL charts, concept maps, event chains, time lines, chains, cycles, and Venn diagrams. The teaching strategy of mnemonics meets the parameters for Bruner's symbolic representation.

In layman's terms, Bruner's enactive learning phase can be linked to kinesthetic learners. The iconic representation phase can be connected with visual learners. Symbolic representation, which involves written and oral language, can be linked to writing/reading and auditory learners from the VARK example in the previous chapter. In essence, Bruner's discovery learning appeals to all learning modalities.

LEV VYGOTSKY—SCAFFOLDING AND ZPDS

Lev Vygotsky (1896–1934) was a Russian theorist whose views on teaching and learning have only recently been implemented in the Western world. It can be confusing to educators to read writings by Vygotsky that were published in the later half of the twentieth century when you see his date of death. Vygotsky's work was translated and shared with the world long after his death. Many of the terms Vygotsky used may sound unusual to us. Please remember that these are translations from Russian. Like Ausubel's advanced or graphic organizers and Bruner's iconic representation, Vygotsky's theory states that learning is facilitated by the use of mental tools that he referred to as *signs*. These signs can include maps, artwork, music, graphics, and the use of symbolic representation using numbers and writing. Signs stimulate the learning process. Translating the concept of signs to learning modalities, signs incorporate the auditory, visual, and kinesthetic learners as well as the writing/reading learners in the VARK example.

Vygotsky was very interested in the student's social interactions. His theory is known as a sociohistorical approach to education, which views learning in the social context rather than isolated behaviors. He believed that "learning is the most effective when children cooperate with one another in a supportive learning environment under the careful guidance of a teacher. Cooperative learning, group problem solving, and cross-age tutoring are instructional strategies used today that have grown in popularity as a result of research evolving from the work of Vygotsky"(Roberts 1996: 13). A fourth instructional strategy might include multiage classrooms. Many educators refer to Vygotsky as the "father of cooperative learning."

Vygotsky believed that learners proceed through four stages of concept attainment: (1) heaps, (2) complexes, (3) potential concepts, and (4) genuine concepts or scientific concepts. Table 3.3 explains in more detail the four stages of concept attainment.

Two cornerstones of Vygotsky's work are the *zone of proximal development* (ZPD) and *scaffolding*. According to Dixon-Krauss (1996: 86), ZPD is the distance between the actual developmental level as determined by independent problem solving and the level of potential development as determined through

Table 3.3. Vygotsky's Four Stages of Concept Attainment

Heaps: Random categories; no relationships; no hierarchy
Example: A car is red. A train goes fast. There is no connection that both are methods of
transportation.

Complexes: Establishes relationships between and among concrete categories
Example: Cars run on roads. Trains run on tracks. Both are modes of transportation.
You can go from here to there in both.

Potential concepts: Students can move from the concrete to the abstract concepts.
Example: Students begin to connect ideas to past experiences. Students develop the
ability to reflect. Students can predict what might happen next. Formal instruction—
teaching beyond direct experience—occurs in this stage. This stage generally lasts
through the remainder of elementary school.

Genuine concepts or scientific concepts: Concepts emerge on the basis of abstract,
systematic knowledge.
Example: The first two stages are the building blocks for the third and fourth stages.

problem solving under adult guidance or in collaboration with more capable peers. ZPD is the space or zone between what a student can learn on his or her own as opposed to what the student is capable of learning when receiving instruction. The instruction may be given from a teacher or a more advanced peer.

According to Maxim (1999), the major implication of ZPD is that teachers must guide by asking timely questions, offering appropriate prompts, and providing stimulating demonstrations. Maxim suggests a teacher–student dialogue similar to the Socratic dialogue in which there is give and take among all participants. Figure 3.1 illustrates the zone of proximal development.

"Scaffolding is the idea of gradually removing the prompts or hints a child needs in order to accomplish some task" (Wolfinger 2000: 48). An example of scaffolding that involves parents is helping a child learn to tie his or her shoe. At first the parent is involved in every phase. Over time, the parent assists only

FIGURE 3.1
Zone of proximal development
Source: Adapted from Ellis (1998)

Learner's Actual Level   Learner's Potential Level

Zone of Proximal Development

when the child needs help. This concept of scaffolding overflows into classrooms each day with new tasks students are required to master. Mastery does not occur the first day. Over time, the teacher's direct role diminishes as the student continues to improve. Teaching someone how to play a musical instrument and teaching computer skills are examples of the teacher's role in the scaffolding process.

Like Bruner, Vygotsky focused on *how* the student learns rather than *what* the student learns. Teaching strategies from the previous chapter that include Vygotsky's view are KWL charts, KWHL charts, event chains, time lines, chains, cycles, Venn diagrams, mnemonics, concept mapping or concept webbing, and cooperative group learning.

HOWARD GARDNER—MULTIPLE INTELLIGENCES

Howard Gardner joined the ranks of the educational theorists when his book *Frames of Mind: The Theory of Multiple Intelligences* was published in 1983. The concept of intelligence had once been only associated with high academic achievers such as Albert Einstein. Gardner's theory supported what teachers have believed for decades—every student brings to the classroom special interests, abilities, talents, gifts, or intelligences. In an institution that too often labels students as high or low achievers, smart or slow, gifted or mentally disabled, Gardner leaves the old labeling system behind. He suggests that "intelligence takes multiple forms and that each individual possesses these forms to a certain degree" (Ellis 1998: 69). As a classroom teacher, you can enhance the intelligences of your students by providing various learning experiences that include all intelligences.

Gardner's eight intelligences may be summarized as follows:

1. *Interpersonal intelligence*: a high level of ability to understand the feelings, desires, and ideas of others
2. *Intrapersonal intelligence*: highly aware of one's self and to be introspective; a self-motivated and independent worker.
3. *Verbal/linguistic intelligence*: a high-level use of language—writing, reading, and speaking
4. *Spatial intelligence*: a high ability to organize the world through spatial relations; interaction with the world through seeing, hearing, tasting, touching, and smelling

5. *Logical/mathematical intelligence*: uses both inductive and deductive reasoning skills and views the world through a mathematical perspective; a high ability to classify, illustrate relationships, and recognize patterns; transfers numbers, symbols, and concepts of mathematics to other curricular areas and the world
6. *Bodily/kinesthetic intelligence*: enhanced learning through movement activities; excels in sports, dance, and other movement activities
7. *Musical intelligence*: a high sensitivity to rhythm, pitch, key, melody, harmony, chords, and timbre; the ability to use the components of music to play and also create new musical forms and compositions
8. *Naturalistic intelligence*: a high sense of the interconnectedness and relationships of the elements of nature; a high interest in such subjects as astronomy, botany, zoology, biology, geology, paleontology, entomology, or meteorology

Teaching strategies from the previous chapter that appeal to Gardner's multiple intelligences include KWL charts, KWHL charts, event chains, time lines, chains, cycles, mnemonics, concept mapping or concept webbing, and cooperative group learning. By designing lessons that enhance your students' multiple intelligences, you will also be designing lessons that include the elements of the three learning modalities.

CONCLUSION

This chapter has given a brief overview of the works of Piaget, Ausubel, Bruner, Vygotsky, and Gardner. The strategies from chapter 2 directly connect to the theories discussed in this chapter.

REFERENCES

Ellis, A. K. 1998. *Teaching and learning elementary social studies.* 6th ed. Boston: Allyn & Bacon.

Dixon-Krauss, L. 1996. *Vygotsky in the classroom.* White Plains, N.Y.: Longman.

Fleer, M. 1992. Identifying teacher–child interaction which scaffolds scientific thinking in young children. *Science Education* 76, no. 4: 393–97.

Heinrich, R., M. Molenda, J. D. Russell, and S. E. Smaldine. 2002. *Instructional media and technologies for learning.* 7th ed. Upper Saddle River, N.J.: Merrill/Prentice Hall.

Maxim, G. M. 1999. *Social studies and the elementary school child.* 6th ed. Upper Saddle River, N.J.: Merrill/Prentice Hall.

Roberts, P. L. 1996. *Integrating language arts and social studies.* Englewood Cliffs, N.J.: Merrill/Prentice Hall.

Wolfinger, D. M. 2000. *Science in the elementary and middle school.* White Plains, N.Y.: Longman.

Additional References

Bruner, J., Rose R. Olver, Patricia M. Greenfield, et al. 1966. *Studies in cognitive growth.* New York: Wiley.

Gardner, H. 1983. *Frames of mind: The theory of multiple intelligences.* New York: Basic Books.

———. 1993. *Multiple intelligences: The theory in practice—a reader.* New York: Basic Books.

Vygotsky, L. S. 1978. *Mind in society.* Cambridge, Mass.: Harvard University Press.

WEB REFERENCES

http://mimas.xsuchoco/edu~ah24/ausubel.htm. Provides Internet information about David Ausubel and his theory.

http://tip.psychology.org/bruner.html. Describes Bruner's constructivist theory.

http://tip.psychology.org/vygotsky.html. Considers Vygotsky's social development theory.

www.uwsp.edu/education/lwilson/learning/3mides.htm. Offers an overview and definitions of the multiple intelligences as well as characteristics found in children.

www.surfaquarium.com/Miinvent.htm. Features an online multiple intelligence survey.

www.dcsd.k12.co.us/elementary/cce/allschol/mi/miinventory.html. Provides an online multiple intelligence test.

www.cdlp.rssd.k12.ca.us.forms/multiple.htm. Presents an online Multiple Intelligence test.

4

Students with an IEP

Today's classrooms are filled with a diversified student body. It is thus no longer reasonable to use the term regular education, *and it is virtually impossible to speak about the "average child" in our classrooms. "In recent years, the range of abilities, handicaps, and socioeconomic circumstances in the regular classroom has posed a significant challenge to teachers" (Van de Walle 1998: 501). As a classroom teacher, you will have a kaleidoscope of students with deficiencies, gifts, and talents spanning the spectrum. According to the Department of Education, nearly 12 percent of students were identified as disabled and had an IEP during the period 1991–1994 (Gega and Peters 1998: 119).*

This chapter is designed for all intended readership groups. Practicing teachers will benefit from a refresher course on the various laws that have impacted American education. The alternative certification and teacher education candidate will benefit from the legal information as well as the information on mainstreaming and inclusion in classrooms today. All groups will see the importance of being part of a collaborative team that decides the best course of education for each child with an IEP, remembering that the I means "individualized."

An individualized educational program (IEP) is developed by a team for a child with specific learning needs. Entire books and college courses address the myriad of special learning problems. Rather than trying to specifically name and elaborate on each area of special education, consider the basics of working with children with an IEP.

PL 94-142

In 1975, the Education for the Handicapped Act (also referred to as the Education for All Handicapped Children Act) set federal guidelines for special education services. Public Law 94-142 was a benchmark for individuals with special needs. Within this act, the categories of disabilities were described, the services to which students might be entitled were specified, and the concept of least restrictive environment was mandated. As an educator, you must be aware of the magnitude and scope of the concept of least restricted environment. This concept is specified in each special needs student's IEP.

PL 99-457

In 1986, Public Law 99-457 was passed. This law specifically extended the provisions of PL 94-142 to very young children—from birth to five years of age. It focused on the family, due to the age of the children and the role parents play at that age. Education plans written under this law were designated individual family service plans.

PL 101-476

The Education for the Handicapped Act (PL 94-142) has since been renamed the Individuals with Disabilities Education Act (IDEA) in 1990. This law (PL 101-476) guarantees a free, appropriate education in the least restrictive environment for students with disabilities, just as did PL 94-142. IDEA changed terminology in which *disability* replaced the word *handicapped*. Other changes included the addition of autism and traumatic brain injury to the categories of disabilities. IDEA provides legal definitions for a wide range of disabilities, including mental disability, specific learning disabilities, and various physical disabilities such as hearing or vision impairment and orthopedic handicaps. In 1991, the law was clarified to include children with attention deficit disorder (ADD) and attention deficit hyperactivity disorder (ADHD).

These three laws made landmark changes in the way special needs children were educated in the United States. Also as a result of these laws, schools were required to become physically accessible to every student. As a visitor to many schools, I have seen the additions of ramps at entry areas, handicapped-accessible restroom facilities, and also disabled-accessible drinking fountains, to name just a few compliances. These changes and many more were necessary for public schools to meet the federal guidelines for special needs students.

INCLUSION AND MAINSTREAMING

Most special education students are taught by using the method or technique of either *inclusion* or *mainstreaming*. Although IDEA provides special services for eligible students, the "least restrictive environment" (often referred to as LRE) is increasingly the regular classroom. The Supreme Court has yet to rule on the LRE provision of IDEA. Lower courts, however, have ruled that school officials must assess whether placement in regular classrooms will benefit the child, not be disruptive to the learning of other students, and be cost-effective (*Devries v. Fairfax County School Board* 1989; *Roncker v. Walter* 1983).

Inclusion refers to placing children with some form of disability in integrated classrooms for the full day. Inclusion brings children of all types into the regular classroom, thus placing a great challenge on the classroom teacher. "As more and more children with special needs are included in regular classrooms, the distinction between special and regular education will soon become obsolete" (Greenes, Garfunkel, and De Bussey 1994: 133).

Inclusion has many benefits to special needs students. "Students who are included, rather than placed into special classes or pulled out of their classroom for special assistance, benefit from having more appropriate instruction and less fragmented educational program" (Wolfinger 2000: 299). Borasi (1994) lists the following advantages for inclusion:

- Regular students serve as learning models for special students.
- Special students frequently offer unique alternative solutions to challenging problems encountered by the full class or in small cooperative groups.
- All students develop an awareness of and respect for individual differences.
- All students, not just the "regular" students, are exposed to good mathematics and challenging experiences.

The American Federation of Teachers (AFT) and the National Education Association (NEA) have reservations about inclusion. The AFT has called for a "moratorium on the placement of disabled children in the regular classroom, while educators review how to more effectively deal with such placements" (Edwards 2000: 344). The NEA more moderately believes that "support for inclusion depends on teachers' receiving appropriate training, being allowed additional time to plan for teaching disabled students, and having class size reduced when disabled students are present" (McCarthy 1994).

"*Mainstreaming* is the placement of developmentally different students in the least restrictive educational environment" (Roberts 1996: 441). A student who is mainstreamed is one who attends special education courses as well as grade-level courses throughout each day. Mainstreaming was part of PL 94-142, which stated in part that the "removal of handicapped children from the regular educational environment occurs only when the nature or severity of the handicap is such that education in regular classes with the use of supplementary aids and services cannot be achieved satisfactorily" (*Federal Register,* August 23, 1997, p. 821). Inclusion or mainstreaming will be specified individually for each child in the IEP.

THE IEP TEAM

Classroom teachers, special educators, parents, counselors, administrators, and paraprofessionals form a collaborative team to determine how to provide the best possible education for all of the special needs students present in the classroom. The collaborative team works to identify the needs of the students, to design educational experiences to meet those needs, to provide assistance in the classroom, and to share their expertise with others. The goal of the collaborative team is to create and approve an IEP. An IEP is a plan developed for an individual child showing the goals, strategies, and evaluative measures that will be used to help the child reach a particular learning or behavioral need. Generally it is designed in an annual goal format, and the collaborative team will meet every year to analyze these goals. The IEP often suggests modifications to classroom instruction that will be needed in working with the student.

"Once the IEP is written and accepted by the collaborative team, it is the teacher's turn. It is up to the teacher to implement the modifications to learning suggested by the IEP" (Cohen 1991). As is often the case, the IEP is designed at the end of the previous school year; therefore, the present classroom teacher usually has no input into the specifications and modifications within the plan—he or she was not part of the collaborative team. If this is your case and you believe that adjustments need to be made within the IEP, as a new member of the collaborative IEP team, you can call a meeting of the team members at any time throughout the school year. Take the time and effort to convene the collaborative team in order for adjustments to be made for the student's best interests.

As an integral part of the collaborative IEP team, take some time to read the plan very well. If you have any questions, discuss them with the special education teacher who helped designed the IEP. Be crystal-clear on your role. Know the modifications, annual goals, and any short-term goals for each of your special needs students.

CONCLUSION

American classrooms today are filled with a myriad of diverse learners. In 1975, the federal government enacted PL 94-142, which set guidelines for special education services. Since that time, other laws have helped fine-tune special education. As a classroom teacher, you will be part of a collaborative team that sets goals for individual students. Your district may favor inclusion or mainstreaming as the best way to educate special needs students.

REFERENCES

Algozzine, B., C. V. Morsink, and K. M. Algozzine. 1988. What's happening in self-contained special education classroom? *Exceptional Children* 55: 259–65.

Borasi, R. 1994, April. Implementing the NCTM Standards in "inclusive" mainstream classrooms. Paper presented at the annual meeting of the National Council of Teachers of Mathematics, Indianapolis.

Cohen, E. 1991. Strategies for creating a multiability classroom. *Cooperative Learning* 12, no. 1: 4–7.

Devries v. Fairfax County School Board, 882 F.2d 876 (4th Cir. 1989).

Edwards, C. H. 2000. *Classroom discipline and management.* 3d ed. New York: Wiley.

Gega, P. C., and J. M. Peters. 1998. *Science in elementary education.* 8th ed. Upper Saddle River, N.J.: Merrill/Prentice Hall.

Greenes, C., F. Garfunkel, and M. De Bussey. 1994. Planning for instructions: The individualized learning plan. In *Windows of opportunity: Mathematics for students with special needs,* ed. C. A. Thornton and N. S. Bley. Reston, Va.: National Council of Teachers of Mathematics, 115–35.

McCarthy, M. M. (1994, November). *Research bulletin. No. 13.* Bloomington, Ind.: Phi Delta Kappa, Center for Evaluation, Development and Research.

Roncker v. Walter, 700 F.2d 1058 (6th Cir. 1983), cert. denied, 464 U.S. 864 (1983).

Roberts, P. L. 1996. *Integrating language arts and social studies for kindergarten and primary children.* Englewood Cliffs, N.J.: Merrill/Prentice Hall.

U.S. Department of Education. 1993. *Fifteenth annual report to Congress on the implementation of the Individuals with Disabilities Education Act.* Washington, D.C.: Author.

Van de Walle, J. 1998. *Elementary and middle school mathematics.* 3d ed. New York: Addison Wesley Longman.

Wolfinger, D. 2000. *Science in elementary and middle school.* New York: Addison Wesley Longman.

Web References

www.sedl.org/change/issues/issues43.html. Offers more information on inclusion.

www.reedmartin.com/courtcases.html. Describes more special education laws.

5

ESL/LEP Students

Two decades ago, only major U.S. cities had students who were not proficient in speaking English. That fact has changed dramatically over the past decade. Within the span of your career, you will have students who are not proficient in English. Please take into consideration that if the student is not proficient, most likely neither are the parents.

National statistics show that 5.2 percent of students in schools today are considered ESL—that is, using English as a second language. Several terms are used to describe these students. This chapter will explore those terms as well as examine the legal case that helped establish bilingual education in the United States.

This chapter is intended for all three readership groups. All readers will benefit from the various terms used to describe students who are not yet proficient in reading, writing, and speaking English. Suggestions and resources are given to help teachers who have ESL students in their classrooms.

The term *ESL* refers to "English as a second language." The ESL movement began to assist non–English-speaking students attending American public schools. The term *LEP* refers to "limited English proficiency." Other terms used throughout education include *LOTE* (language other than English), *ELL* (English language learner), and *NOM* (national origin minority). Because the government uses ESL and LEP for classification purposes, those terms will be used throughout this segment. There is no intent to use these terms in a negative or demeaning fashion to any individual or group. Whichever term you use, the goal is to teach content curriculum to limited-English-speaking students to the best of your ability—so every student will learn.

The landmark court case that established bilingual education in America was *Lau v. Nichols* (414 U.S.563 [1974]). This suit was brought by non-English-speaking Chinese students against officials responsible for the operation of the San Francisco Unified School District. *Lau* did for bilingual education what *Brown v. Board of Education* did for the "separate is not equal" issue. The U.S. Supreme Court ruled in *Brown* that separate schools for African American children were not equal to the separate schools for white children; thus, schools began to integrate. Both *Brown* and *Lau* were decided in the Supreme Court rather than through a constitutional amendment. The following is a summary of the *Lau* ruling:

> When children arrive in school with little or no English-speaking ability, "sink or swim" instruction is a violation of their civil rights, according to the U.S. Supreme Court in this 1974 decision. *Lau* remains the major precedent regarding the educational rights of language minorities, although it is grounded in statute (Title VI of the Civil Rights Act of 1964), rather than in the U.S. Constitution. At issue was whether school administrators may meet their obligation to provide equal educational opportunities merely by treating all students the same, or whether they must offer special help for students unable to understand English. Lower federal courts had absolved the San Francisco school district of any responsibility for minority children's "language deficiency." But a unanimous Supreme Court disagreed. Its ruling opened a new era in federal civil rights enforcement under the so-called "Lau Remedies." The decision was delivered by Justice William O. Douglas on January 21, 1974. (www.ourworld.compuserve.com/homepages/JWCRAWFORD/lau.htm)

Savage and Armstrong (2000) believe that pupils need two types of language proficiency to succeed in content-area classes:

> One of these focuses on the development of *basic interpersonal communication skills*. This is what they use to communicate on the playground, in the store, or elsewhere to convey their needs. The second type of language proficiency is termed *cognitive/academic language proficiency*. This kind of language expertise allows pupils to understand and communicate in classroom discussions where the contextual clues are reduced and where unique terminology is used. (475)

As a classroom teacher, you should take note of the two types of language proficiency. Just because a student can communicate with peers in the cafeteria does not guarantee that he or she will be able to complete higher-level thinking tasks in the classroom. According to Savage and Armstrong (2000), sometimes teachers make the mistake of assuming that because a pupil has developed a fairly high degree of basic interpersonal communication skill, he or she also possesses a high level of cognitive/academic language proficiency. It usually takes students whose first language is not English several years to acquire a cognitive/academic language proficiency similar or equivalent to that of a native speaker of English. As a classroom teacher, you should set high expectations for every student; however, understand the abilities and inabilities of your ESL or LEP students. They will progress each day toward the goal of the cognitive/academic language proficiency level.

Public schools take one of two approaches to ESL or LEP students. One approach uses bilingual classrooms to teach students in their native language or in both English and their native language. As students progress along the continuum toward English proficiency, they are mainstreamed during parts of the day into the all-English-speaking classrooms. Savage and Armstrong (2000) refer to this method as *additive bilingualism*. Additive bilingualism occurs when individuals learn a new language with little or no pressure to reduce their first language and culture. "Students who experience additive programs have a more positive self-concept than those who experience subtractive programs" (475).

A second approach is *total immersion* in which non-English- or limited-English-speaking students are placed in all-English-speaking classes. They are immersed in English. Savage and Armstrong (2000) refer to this method as *subtractive bilingualism*. Subtractive bilingualism occurs when there is pressure to replace or demote the first language and culture.

Whichever approach your district advocates, consider the four modes of language when working with an ESL or LEP student. According to Kellough (1996), individuals first communicate by listening, then speaking, followed by reading, and finally writing. The same progression will be true for students learning another language.

Another language acquisition model is that designed by Terrell (1981). The four stages, according to Terrell, are based on what has been termed the *natural approach* to language development. Terrell's stages include preproduction, early production, emergence of speech, and intermediate fluency. The following description of Terrell's (1981) stages will be helpful to classroom teachers:

- The *preproduction stage* is often found among people from non-English-speaking countries who have recently arrived in the United States. The name of the stage is based on the idea that even though these individuals may know a few English words, they are too shy to respond and generally prefer to remain silent. They often point or gesture to communicate.
- In the *early production stage*, individuals begin to try limited production of the language. These individuals may have a receptive vocabulary of about one thousand words but can produce only about 10 percent of these. This stage may last from six months to one year.
- In the *emergence of speech stage*, individuals begin to feel more comfortable with the language and are more willing to attempt to speak sentences and participate in conversations. They have broadened their receptive vocabulary to about seven thousand words, with about 10 percent production. Pupils who have arrived at this stage of language proficiency can begin to participate in group writing activities and in reading literature they select themselves.
- The *intermediate fluency stage* often takes pupils three or four years to attain. At this stage, individuals engage in everyday conversations with ease. Pupils have developed a fairly high level of development in the language domains of listening and speaking. Remember that the pupils' level of language proficiency in some areas is likely to fall short of that of native speakers of English. Often because many pupils speak the language well, teachers may confuse verbal fluency with total mastery of the language. As a classroom teacher, remember that these pupils are being asked to learn content presented in a language in which many have not yet attained native speakers' fluency.

We know that ESL or LEP students benefit from portfolio assessments (see chapter 14, "Student Portfolios"). We also know that ESL or LEP students benefit from cooperative group leaning activities, such as those promoted by Lev Vygotsky (see chapter 3). Savage and Armstrong (2000) believe that classroom teachers can enhance the learning of ESL or LEP students by implementing the so-called affective filter.

The key element in providing a classroom environment where second language learning is enhanced in the *social-emotional component*. This is what experts in language acquisition call the *affective filter*. The affective filter refers to the combination of the affective variables of self-concept, motivation, anxiety, and fear that can facilitate or block language learning. The climate of the classroom interacts with these variables to raise or lower the affective filter. It is hypothesized that when the affective filter is high or when there is a great deal of anxiety or threat, a pupil has trouble processing information that would be comprehensible if the affective filter were lower.

For the teacher of limited-English-proficient pupils, this implies that the classroom climate needs to be a safe and an encouraging one. Teachers need to use positive reinforcement and celebrate pupils' successes. They must be careful when correcting pupils so that the student does not develop a fear of ridicule or failure. Teachers and English-proficient pupils in the classroom need to model acceptance and encourage linguistically different learners. (480)

Working with an ESL or LEP student can be overwhelming for both the student and the teacher. Gega and Peters (1998: 123) offer ten suggestions to assist you as a classroom teacher:

- Use a listening-speaking-reading-writing sequence in teaching. This is similar to the model suggested by Kellough (1996).
- Use multisensory, hands-on teaching methods.
- Pair LEP students with bilingual partners or in cooperative learning groups.
- Speak slowly, use short sentences, and rephrase. Use body language, props, pictures, and sketches for clarification.
- Check understanding by asking questions answered by yes or no.
- Avoid idiomatic expressions.
- Be as concrete as possible.
- Write key concepts and vocabulary used during a lesson on the chalkboard to assist in building schemata.
- Emphasize and repeat key words.
- Make language experience charts.

As a classroom teacher, you need to be aware of the opportunities available for your ESL or LEP students. If you have a student who is not proficient in speaking English, what avenues does the district have to best benefit that student? If the student is not proficient in speaking English, most likely neither are the parents. How will you communicate with the parents, either verbally at a conference or in written form? Again, how will the district assist you? In most cases, the district will have a school board–approved policy to assist you in providing the best possible education for the student.

Outside the realm of public schools lies a great source of support: places of worship in the area. Pastors, priests, and rabbis know their members well. Leaders from various religious groups can be a great asset to help you in locating an adult to act as a translator when communicating with the parents of your non-English-speaking student. They have access to a wide variety of individuals within their organizations. If you have located a translator through the private sector, notify your administrator. Be certain that you have his or her approval to utilize this individual in the capacity of communicating confidential student information to the student's parents. The district may have special waiver forms for the parents to sign prior to the conferences with an interpreter.

Consider communicating with LEP or ESL parents by using technology. Numerous computer programs can translate the English text you type instantly into a myriad of language choices. This technology could be used to send home communications, such as school newsletters or teacher communications. Technology could also be utilized during your parent–teacher conferences by typing your information onto the computer screen and instantly translating it for the parent to read. If your district has numerous students and parents who are limited English speaking, suggest the purchase of a program and obtain a site license so all teachers at your school site have access to this opportunity. As with any purchase of technology, survey all the options, and select a program that best meets the needs of your school.

Suppose you have one or more ESL or LEP students in your classes this year. What is your next step? You can contact your district and area churches for assistance. You can also check national organizations to learn about further assistance for you and your ESL students.

Several regional resource centers for bilingual education are located throughout the United States. These centers offer training and technical support services to schools. For the center closest to you or for additional information regarding teaching non-English-proficient students, please contact:

National Clearinghouse for Bilingual Education, 1118 22d Street, N.W., Washington, D.C. 20037; phone: (800) 321-6223

Another source of reference is the website for the Teachers of English to Speakers of Other Languages (TESOL): www.tesol.org. TESOL is a national organization for educators with an interest in helping improve the English-language proficiency of people who are nonnative speakers of English. This site links to other websites with information that can help teachers who teach learners for whom English is a second language.

CONCLUSION

Lau v. Nichols was the landmark court case regarding non-English-speaking public school students. The result was two approaches designed to teach LEP or ESL students. Just as major efforts have been made to best teach ESL students, suggestions were given in this chapter for the teacher to communicate with non-English-speaking parents.

REFERENCES

Baker, C. 1996. *Foundations of bilingual education and bilingualism.* 2d ed. Philadelphia: Multilingual Matters.

Gega, P. C., and J. M. Peters 1998. *Science in elementary education.* 8th ed. Upper Saddle River, N.J.: Merrill/Prentice Hall.

Kellough, R. D. 1996. *Integrating language arts and social studies for intermediate and middle school students.* Englewood Cliffs, N.J.: Merrill/Prentice Hall.

Savage, T. V., and D. G. Armstrong. 2000. *Effective teaching in elementary social studies.* 4th ed. Englewood Cliffs, N.J.: Merrill/Prentice Hall.

Terrell, T. 1981. The natural approach in bilingual education. In *Schooling and language minority students: A theoretical framework,* ed. California State Department of Education. Los Angeles: California State University, Los Angeles Evaluation and Assessment Center of Education, 117–46.

WEB REFERENCES

www.ncbe.gwu.edu/askncbe/faqs/10terms.htm. Provides a glossary of terms and acronyms.

www.ncbe.gwu.edu/ncbepubs/projects/state-data/. Cites state K–12 LEP enrollment and top languages.

www.ncbe.gwu.edu/askncbe/faqs/01leps.htm. Provides the number of school-age LEP students in the United States.

www.ed.gov/offices/OCR/docs/laumemos.html. Presents the policy memoranda on the schools' obligations toward national origin minority students who are LEP ("Lau Memoranda").

www.ncbe.gwu.edu/. The National Clearinghouse maintains this site for bilingual education with funds provided by the U.S. Department of Education's Office of Bilingual Education and Minority Languages Affairs. It contains information of interest to teachers who work with learners who are not native speakers of English. Also included are links to other relevant sites.

http://cisl.ospi.wednet.edu/CISL/Strategies/CRSAGETUTR.html. Includes a list of ERIC Document Reproduction Service documents and articles in educational journals that focus on approaches to assisting LEP pupils by using cross-age tutoring techniques. Also included are links to relevant sites.

http://esl.net/. Seattle-based ESL Net is an information source for materials of all kinds on English as a second language; offers direct links to schools with strong ESL programs.

ADDRESSING STUDENT NEEDS

Mrs. Smith's Fifth-Grade Class Calendar	
Monday **April 3**	Begin new chapter in social studies—chapter 16, "America Moves West." Spelling bonus words for week: vertebrate, invertebrate, mollusk, echinoderm
Tuesday **April 4**	
Wednesday **April 5**	Science exam covering chapter 12, "Invertebrates"; study questions were sent home Friday, March 29.
Thursday **April 6**	Assembly in the gym—Freddie the Friendly Firehouse Clown—at 10:00 A.M.; parents and family are invited.
Friday **April 7**	Spelling test—chapter 38 Calendar for following week, corrected papers, and science test go home tonight.

Best practice refers to situations or ideas that are not necessarily theory based but are agreed on in educational circles. Throughout Part I, you have learned ways to best address your students' needs. One final suggestion focuses on a situation that occurs often in classrooms—the new student. The tips in this final section will help you welcome a new student to your classroom and your school site.

Many school sites have a "New Student Folder" that can be presented when a new individual arrives throughout the year. This folder is a great tool for children entering the district for the first time or transferring to your site from another within the district.

If your school does not have a "New Student Folder," consider necessary information that could be easily packaged for you to send home. You might use a manila folder or a large yellow envelope. The contents could include some of the following suggestions:

- Student handbook
- List of breakfast or lunch prices
- School calendar
- Student supply list

A convenient way to assimilate the student into your routine is to ask several boys or girls to "shadow" the new student for the first week. Realize that this new student doesn't know the geography of the school, the class schedule, and so forth. Shadowing by several students will help promote friendships and build confidence.

Perhaps the most important phone call you make during the school year will be to the parent of a new student in your classroom. This was always my most enjoyable phone call of the year. I "batted a thousand" because *every* parent was truly appreciative and grateful that I had taken the time to contact them.

Consider making a parent phone call after the student has attended for several days. The parents will have had time to receive feedback from their child during the evenings. Just as a new student has questions, a new parent will also have questions regarding the classroom and the school. As with all parental phone calls, maintain confidentiality of all students.

Your efforts to make a new student welcome will pay high dividends to the newcomer, your classroom, and your school. Make the efforts.

AWAKENING GENIUS IN THE CLASSROOM

One area that was not addressed in this section was that of the genius. Armstrong (1998) believes that every child is a genius. He has established twelve qualities of the genius: "curiosity, playfulness, imagination, creativity, wonder, wisdom, inventiveness, vitality, sensitivity, flexibility, humor, and joy" (2–3).

Armstrong believes that as teachers we must provide ways to continue to inspire our students' genius abilities. He also suggests that the teacher must make efforts to rekindle the genius within ourselves.

Reading Armstrong's book will take about two hours of your day. It will, however, linger in your mind and rekindle the flame of teaching in your heart for a much longer time.

REFERENCE

Armstrong, T. 1998. *Awakening genius in the classroom.* Alexandria, Va.: Association for Supervision and Curriculum Development.

II

THE ESSENTIALS OF PROFESSIONALISM: PLANNING

Teachers make hundreds of decisions throughout the day. Part II offers suggestions to streamline the lesson plan book to best meet the individualized needs of your classroom. While you are planning, utilizing the cognitive, psychomotor, and affective domains, a substitute folder is essential. Detailed recommendations are also given for setting up and maintaining a substitute folder.

In the process of planning your daily lessons each day, keep foremost in your mind the purpose of education. Plan lessons that will stimulate and ignite your students to the passion of the topic. Consider all possible options from the strategies from Part I to best help your students LEARN. Bruner and others focused on *how* students learn. Keep that issue in mind when planning. Write the following phrase from the poet Robert Frost in your lesson plan book, and refer to it often, commit it to memory, make it part of your daily repertoire: "I am not a teacher but an awakener."

6

Lesson Plan Book

This chapter discusses the importance of the lesson plan book as well as ideas for thinking outside the box and designing your own book. Teacher education candidates will benefit from this chapter as an overview and preview to the time when they have their own classroom and their own lesson plan book. For teachers already in the field, no matter where you are in the school year, you can take this information and tailor it to best meet the individualized needs of your classroom.

Every principal on the planet has a different requirement for content and substance of lesson plans. Some administrators want details listing everything except "chapter and verse." Some principals review the lesson plan books every week. Some never look at them. Why, then, are lesson plans so very important? The following information will shed light on their significance.

Writing lesson plans and keeping the lesson plan book current will comprise some form of your professional evaluation. In Oklahoma, for example, first-year teachers are evaluated in four areas: human relations, teaching and assessment, classroom management, and professionalism. As a university representative, I am part of a team that makes periodic evaluations of first-year teachers. Under the classroom management portion of our evaluation instrument includes "Writes lesson plans designed to achieve the identified objectives." I check the plan book cover to cover, as do the other members of the evaluation team.

The heart and soul of good lesson plans is good decision making. You must decide the objectives of the lesson (see the next chapter, "The 'Big Three

Domains,'" for more ideas on objectives), how you will teach the lesson, and how you will assess the objectives. Each state has a set of objectives that must be attained for each subject level at each grade level. There are also national *standards* for each curricular area. You will also have specific objectives that you believe must be achieved in each lesson. Your decisions are endless.

Your lesson plans are an important and useful part of your daily routine as a classroom teacher. Kellough (1996: 94) lists several benefits of lesson plans:

- Lesson plans give a teacher an agenda or outline to follow in teaching a lesson.
- They give a substitute teacher a basis for presenting appropriate lessons to a class.
- They provide the teacher with something to fall back on in case of memory lapse, an interruption, or some other distraction, such as a call from the office or a fire drill.

Kellough (1996) believes that the most important benefit of lesson plans is "they provide beginners with security, because with a carefully prepared plan a beginning teacher can walk into a classroom with the confidence gained from having developed a sensible framework for that day's instruction" (94). Kellough adds that written lesson plans show that thinking and planning have taken place and that the teacher has a road map to work through the lesson no matter what the distractions.

Take the initiative to learn exactly what details your administrator requires before you begin writing in your lesson plans. I would encourage you to visit with other teachers at your grade level or subject area about their lesson plan books. Also ask your principal for examples of acceptable plans. Often teachers do not turn in plan books at the end of the year; therefore, one of the seasoned professionals may have an old book for you to look over to see what is expected of you.

Several models for lesson plans are available. The web references at the end of this chapter list several sites to learn more about Madeline Hunter's "Elements of Effective Instruction" or Robert Gagne's "Nine Instructional Events." Both are good models to view and reflect upon. As a university methods professor, my students often ask what is the best model for a lesson plan. I believe that the simpler the better. No teacher ever has enough time during the day. If the lesson plan or instructional format is simple, a teacher can consistently in-

Table 6.1.   Lesson Plan/Instructional Format

Objective: Use a measurable objective.
Introduction: Give overview: how will you start? Any background information? Connect today's lesson to the content of yesterday's.
Instruction: Describe content—briefly, *what* are you teaching, and *how* are you teaching the concept?
Guided practice/independent practice: This relates to the activity for the lesson. Is this a cooperative group activity? Is this age group capable of cooperative group activities? Is this an individual assignment or project? Small-group activity? Whole-group assignment? *How* will the students learn?
Assessment: How will you put a grade in the grade book over this lesson? (Part III will give additional information on the assessment portion.)
Closure: How will you wrap up this lesson or project? If possible, connect lesson to content of tomorrow's lesson by giving one-sentence review and preview.

clude all the elements. Table 6.1 presents the format that I use with my elementary science, language arts, social studies, and mathematics methods courses—the same format for all courses. You might wish to modify or adapt this format.

Each component of the format is vital to effective teaching and, most important, student learning. No single part is more important than the others. Many would debate that the instruction is the most important element of a lesson. I believe that no man is an island; thus, no portion is able to stand alone. All parts are needed to help students learn.

Whether your principal requires sketchy or well-detailed lesson plans, you will be required to write down daily plans in a lesson plan book. Always write your plans in pencil rather than in ink. Flexibility is a wonderful quality in any teacher. You may need to adjust your plans due to an unexpected assembly, a day missed due to inclement weather, or just because your students need an extra day of reteaching. Whatever the case, you can always erase penciled plans and adjust your plan book. Attempting to adjust or rewrite plans written in ink would be much more difficult.

Because your days will be well structured to meet the needs of your students, consider designing your own personalized lesson plan book. My final years in elementary school were in a departmentalized setting. I only taught three subjects twice daily; therefore, I only needed three plans per day. As a third-grade teacher, however, I required two lesson plan books in order to include the three math groups and four reading groups I had within my classroom as well as all the other curricular areas. Every teacher has a unique teaching assignment. Efforts to personalize the lesson plan book will save time and help the days in the classroom run more smoothly.

Consider designing a plan grid with five quadrants running vertically (for the five days of the week) and the number of curricular areas you need *plus one* running horizontally. The last vertical column will be a space to write in your agenda—the special things you have each day such as cafeteria times, recess, and special classes such as gym, music, or computer lab. You can also use the last column to write in any special events such as Picture Day or an assembly one day that week. Table 6.2 shows an example.

Table 6.3 presents a sample of a single-page lesson plan book for a middle school or high school teacher. Table 6.4 is a sample of a two-page lesson plan

Table 6.2.   Daily Plans for a Departmentalized Teaching Schedule

Math	Science	Social Studies	Agenda
Monday			
The students will be able to:	The students will be able to:	The students will be able to:	Gym/Music/ Computer 10:00–10:45
Notes:	Notes:	Notes:	
			Lunch
Assignment:	Assignment:	Assignment:	12:00/12:10/12:15
Tuesday			
The students will be able to:	The students will be able to:	The students will be able to:	Gym/Music/ Computer 10:00–10:45
Notes:	Notes:	Notes:	
			Lunch
Assignment:	Assignment:	Assignment:	12:00/12:10/12:15
Wednesday			
The students will be able to:	The students will be able to:	The students will be able to:	Gym/Music/ Computer 10:00–10:45
Notes:	Notes:	Notes:	
			Lunch
Assignment:	Assignment:	Assignment:	12:00/12:10/12:15 Library 1:00–1:30
Thursday			
The students will be able to:	The students will be able to:	The students will be able to:	Gym/Music/ Computer 10:00–10:45
Notes:	Notes:	Notes:	
			Spanish 9:15–9:45
Assignment:	Assignment:	Assignment:	Lunch 12:00/12:10/12:15

Table 6.2. *(continued)*

Math	Science	Social Studies	Agenda
Friday			
The students will be able to:	The students will be able to:	The students will be able to:	Gym/Music/ Computer 10:00–10:45
Notes:	Notes:	Notes:	
Assignment:	Assignment:	Assignment:	Lunch 12:00/12:10/12:15 *3:00 pass out popcorn

Table 6.3. **Personalized Plan Book—Single Page**

1st Hour 7:30–8:25 World History	2d Hour 8:30–9:25 U.S. History	3d Hour 10:30–11:25 Geography	4th Hour 12:00–12:55 U.S.History	5th Hour 1:00–1:55 World History	6th Hour 2:00–2:55 World History
Monday					
The students will be able to: **Parking lot Duty A.M.**	The students will be able to:	The students will be able to:	The students will be able to:	The students will be able to:	The students will be able to:
Tuesday					
The students will be able to:	The students will be able to:	The students will be able to:	The students will be able to: **Noon cafeteria duty**	The students will be able to:	The students will be able to:
Wednesday					
The students will be able to:	The students will be able to:	The students will be able to:	The students will be able to:	The students will be able to:	The students will be able to: **Practice chess club 3:00**
Thursday					
The students will be able to:	The students will be able to:	The students will be able to:	The students will be able to:	The students will be able to:	The students will be able to:
Friday					
The students will be able to:	The students will be able to:	The students will be able to:	The students will be able to:	The students will be able to:	The students will be able to:

Table 6.4.   Personalized Plan Book—Two Pages

1st Hour 7:30–8:25 World History	2d Hour 8:30–9:25 U.S. History	3d Hour 10:30–11:25 Geography
The students will be able to:	The students will be able to:	The students will be able to:
Notes:	Notes:	Notes:
Assignment:	Assignment:	Assignment:
Monday The students will be able to:	The students will be able to:	The students will be able to:
Notes:	Notes:	Notes:
Assignment:	Assignment:	Assignment:
Tuesday The students will be able to:	The students will be able to:	The students will be able to:
Notes:	Notes:	Notes:
Assignment:	Assignment:	Assignment:
Wednesday The students will be able to:	The students will be able to:	The students will be able to:
Notes:	Notes:	Notes:
Assignment:	Assignment:	Assignment:
Thursday The students will be able to:	The students will be able to:	The students will be able to:
Notes:	Notes:	Notes:
Assignment:	Assignment:	Assignment:
Friday The students will be able to:	The students will be able to:	The students will be able to:
Notes:	Notes:	Notes:
Assignment:	Assignment:	Assignment:

book for a middle school or high school teacher. One page will be on the left side and one on the right when the lesson plan book is opened.

Once you've designed your lesson plan book, type or write in the necessary information such as "Reading 9:00–10:00" as a heading for that quadrant for all five days. Continue to add the information for each quadrant. Leave room

Table 6.4. *(continued)*

4th Hour 12:00-12:55 U.S. History	5th Hour 1:00-1:55 World History	6th Hour 2:00-2:55 World History	Agenda
The students will be able to:	The students will be able to:	The students will be able to:	Parking lot duty 7:00-7:20
Notes:	Notes:	Notes:	
Assignment:	Assignment:	Assignment:	
Monday			
The students will be able to:	The students will be able to:	The students will be able to:	*Meet with Chess* *Club. 3:00.* *Room 441B*
Notes:	Notes:	Notes:	
Assignment:	Assignment:	Assignment:	
Tuesday			
The students will be able to:	The students will be able to:	The students will be able to:	Cafeteria duty
Notes:	Notes:	Notes:	
Assignment:	Assignment:	Assignment:	
Wednesday			
The students will be able to:	The students will be able to:	The students will be able to:	*Department meeting*
Notes:	Notes:	Notes:	
Assignment:	Assignment:	Assignment:	
Thursday			
The students will be able to:	The students will be able to:	The students will be able to:	
Notes:	Notes:	Notes:	
Assignment:	Assignment:	Assignment:	
Friday			

to write in your plans in the space provided—remember, you will write those plans in pencil. Take this to your principal for approval. Make any changes he or she suggests, and then send it back again if necessary for additional approval. When you have the green light to proceed, take your pages to the copying machine and create your own plan book. You may hole-punch the pages and put them in a three-ring binder, or you may wish to take it to your local photocopying business and have it bound so it will open out flat. Either choice will provide an efficient, time-saving book that will best help meet the needs of your classroom for that school year. Save your personally designed lesson plan information on a diskette or on your computer hard drive. If you have teaching assignment changes for next year, they can be easily adjusted from the saved changes from this year.

I used icons in the far right vertical quadrant for gym, music, and computer lab. My students rotated among those pull-outs each day at a specified time. I was able to use a colored magic marker and highlight the appropriate pull-out icon for the correct day. It took a few seconds to prepare this section for the next week. My colleagues were writing in the names of each pull-out for each day—for 180 days. My method saved much time throughout the school year.

You may wish to use icons throughout your plan book, but have a "key" so that the substitute knows what each symbol means. This key can be part of your Substitute Folder (see chapter 9 for additional information). Always examine your plans to be sure that another individual could pick them up and teach the lessons in case you are absent. Use your talents and abilities to your advantage to help you save one of life's most precious gifts—time!

Numerous websites can assist you in preparing lesson plans. The information listed under "Web References" is not even the tip of the Internet iceberg. You will develop your own repertoire of favorite websites as the school year progresses. You will also learn about sites from colleagues. Surf the Internet for great resources to enhance learning for your students.

REFERENCE

Kellough, R. D. 1996. *Integrating mathematics and science for intermediate and middle school students.* Englewood Cliffs, N.J.: Merrill/Prentice Hall.

WEB REFERENCES

http://ericir.syr.edu. Provides a wide variety of lesson plans that are organized by major school subjects. There are also links to other sites that feature additional lesson plans. At the university, we refer to this site as "Ask ERIC."

http://school.discovery.com/. This site is provided by the Discovery Channel. Look for *"Classroom Activities."*

http://ed.info.apple.com/education/techlearn/lessonmenu.html. Includes links to lesson plans prepared by the Apple K–12 education program, organized according to elementary schools, middle schools, and high schools.

www.pbs.org/teachersource/

www.proteacher.com/

www.school.discovery.com/

www.lessonplanspage.com/index.html

http://bookadventure.com/te/bkt/te_bkt_tl_tt.asp

http://crayola.com/educators/index.cfm. Offers a wealth of art ideas. You can specify the age group with which you are working.

www.keele.ac.ul/depts/cs/Stephen_Bostock/docs/atid.htm. The site for Robert Gagné's "Nine Instructional Events."

http://tip.psychology.org/gagne.html. Provides additional information about Gagné's theories.

www.humbolt.edu/~tha1/hunter-eei.htm/. Discusses Madeline Hunter's "Elements of Effective Instruction."

www.uoregon.edu/~christyk/ssm/hunter.html. Offers Hunter's lesson plan templates.

www.msu.edu/~zeneber1/itip.htm. Discusses Hunter's ideas on "Effective Instruction."

7

The "Big Three Domains"

Every teacher education major worth his or her salt must learn the three learning domains. This chapter not only discusses the domains but connects them to verbs that can be used by any teacher when writing teaching objectives. The cornerstone of the cognitive domain—Bloom's taxonomy—is discussed along with taxonomies for the affective and psychomotor domains. If you are a teacher education candidate, the information in this chapter will be a good resource for you to use with your courses. If you are an alternative certification candidate or a practicing teacher, you will learn valuable verbs to use when writing your teaching objectives. My students and also first-year teachers use this information as "cheat sheets" when writing their objectives.

There are three major domains used to classify learning: cognitive, affective, and psychomotor. The *cognitive* domain, most often used in educational settings, involves mental thought. An example of a lesson involving the cognitive domain would be recalling the date or persons connected in the Jamestown colony. The *affective* domain involves values, feelings, and attitudes. An affective lesson could include some aspect of music or art appreciation. Many character education programs target or focus on the affective domain, as do religious-affiliated private schools. The *psychomotor* domain focuses on physical manipulation or physical actions. An example of a psychomotor lesson could be baking muffins, performing a science experiment, or building a birdhouse. More performance-based courses such as home economics, woodworking, computer science, instrumental music, and physical education would use many objectives within the psychomotor realm.

As educators, and especially as beginning educators, use *measurable* objectives when writing your lesson plans. Verbs that are ambiguous or open to interpretation will also be impossible to determine. We would all like for the students to *enjoy, appreciate, or perceive,* but those verbs open the door to problems to determine specifically whether the objectives have been met by every student. Avoid like a bad plague the following verbs when creating your lesson plans:

> "The students will be able to comprehend, believe, grasp, understand, think, have a knowledge of, increase interest in, become acquainted with, sympathize with, have faith in, or develop an understanding of . . . ."

Another frequently used verb to avoid is *know.* Individuals inexperienced in writing objectives will frequently use this verb. How will you assess or measure if every student "knows" the information? If less than 100 percent "know" the concept, what will you teach tomorrow? "Know" is very difficult to measure on a daily assignment. This example can have measurable verbs substituted for solid teaching objectives. In the next example, *diagram* is both measurable and an action verb.

> **Example:** "The students will be able to diagram a concept map or web showing four habitats or biomes in North America."

With this approach, the teacher can both see the completed work and measure it for a grade. If the student can only use three habitats or biomes in the diagram, it is obvious and evident that this student needs more reteaching. By designating a point value for each habitat, assigning a grade for this assignment will be much easier.

Bloom's taxonomy is widely used in describing different types of cognitive behavior. A *taxonomy* is a system of hierarchical classification, rather than a continuum classification. Bloom's taxonomy is organized into six levels, each representing a more complex type of cognitive thinking or behavior. Starting with the simplest and moving to the most complex, the six levels are *knowledge, comprehension, application, analysis, synthesis,* and *evaluation.*

The Bloom's taxonomy is a good reference when writing objectives for lesson plans. Too often teachers use lower-level objectives such as *list*, *match*, *select*, *name*, *define*, *identify*, *repeat*, and so on. Since it is more difficult to describe student performance for higher-level behaviors, there is a tendency to state the majority of one's educational objectives in terms of lower-level, memory-oriented behaviors. Table 7.1 shows terms that can be used to describe performances more complicated than simple recall.

Many educators will refer to an area of Bloom's taxonomy as a "lower level" or a "higher level." Table 7.2 illustrates Bloom's information as a hierarchy with the lowest level of the taxonomy at the bottom. This view is often much easier for teachers to understand.

If you are a primary teacher, your students *can* attain the evaluation objectives in August verbally but not necessarily in written form. Don't sell those primary students short. Include evaluation objectives in your plans, but specify that they will *verbally relate* or *verbally summarize*. Perhaps the most frequent mistake teachers make when designing teaching objectives is underestimating the abilities of their class. They set the "bar for achievement" too low. For example, they dwell in the knowledge area rather than moving to higher-order thinking objectives. Even a four-year-old can *group* or *combine*. Set your bar for achievement in the realm of the stars.

Table 7.1.   Bloom's Taxonomy—Lateral

Knowledge	Comprehension	Application	Analysis	Synthesis	Evaluation
Count	Classify	Change	Diagram	Arrange	Appraise
Define	Compare	Compute	Differentiate	Combine	Conclude
Identify	Convert	Construct	Discriminate	Compile	Contrast
Label	Contrast	Demonstrate	Outline	Construct	Critique
List	Discuss	Illustrate	Relate	Create	Criticize
Match	Distinguish	Predict	Separate	Design	Grade
Name	Estimate	Relate	Subdivide	Formulate	Judge
Outline	Explain	Solve		Generalize	Justify
Point out	Generalize			Generate	Interpret
Quote	Give examples			Group	Support
Recite	Infer			Integrate	Recommend
Repeat	Interpret			Organize	
Reproduce	Paraphrase			Relate	
Select	Rewrite			Summarize	
State	Summarize				
Trace	Translate				

Source: Adapted from Kellough (1996).

Table 7.2. Bloom's Taxonomy—Certical

Evaluation	Synthesis	Analysis	Application	Comprehension	Knowledge
Appraise	Arrange	Diagram	Change	Classify	Count
Conclude	Combine	Differentiate	Compute	Compare	Define
Contrast	Compile	Discriminate	Construct	Convert	Identify
Critique	Construct	Outline	Demonstrate	Contrast	Label
Grade	Create	Relate	Illustrate	Discuss	List
Judge	Design	Separate	Predict	Distinguish	Match
Justify	Formulate	Subdivide	Relate	Estimate	Name
Interpret	Generalize		Solve	Explain	Outline
Support	Generate			Generalize	Point out
Recommend	Group			Give examples	Quote
	Integrate			Infer	Recite
	Organize			Interpret	Repeat
	Relate			Paraphrase	Reproduce
	Summarize			Rewrite	Select
				Summarize	State
				Translate	Trace

Source: Adapted from Kellough (1996).

Table 7.3. Affective Domain Hierarchy

Receiving	Responding	Valuing	Organizing	Internalizing Values
Ask	Answer	Argue	Adhere	Act
Choose	Applaud	Assist	Alter	Complete
Describe	Approve	Complete	Arrange	Display
Differentiate	Assist	Describe	Balance	Influence
Distinguish	Comply	Differentiate	Combine	Listen
Hold	Command	Explain	Compare	Modify
Identify	Discuss	Follow	Defend	Perform
Locate	Greet	Form	Define	Practice
Name	Help	Initiate	Discuss	Propose
Point to	Label	Invite	Explain	Qualify
Recall	Perform	Join	Form	Question
Recognize	Play	Justify	Generalize	Revise
Reply	Practice	Propose	Identify	Serve
Select	Present	Protest	Integrate	Solve
Use	Read	Read	Modify	Verify
	Recite	Report	Order	
	Report	Select	Organize	
	Select	Share	Prepare	
	Spend (leisure time in)	Study	Relate	
	Tell	Support	Synthesize	
	Write	Work		

Source: Adapted from Krathwohl, Bloom, and Marisa (1964).

Table 7.4. Psychomotor Hierarchy

Movement	Gross-motor coordination Verbs = *adjust, carry, clean, locate, obtain, walk* *Sample objective:* The student will be able to manipulate a hand-held calculator.
Manipulation	Fine-motor coordination Verbs = *assemble, build, calibrate, connect, thread* *Sample objective:* The student will be able to focus the microscope correctly.
Communicating	Communication of ideas and feelings Verbs = *analyze, ask, describe, draw, explain, write* *Sample objective:* The student will be able to draw accurate details of what is depicted while observing a prepared slide through the microscope.
Creating	Represents student's coordination of thinking, learning, and behaving Verbs = *create, design, invent* Sample objective: The student will be able to use discarded materials from the environment to design an environment for an imaginary animal that he or she has mentally created.

Source: Adapted from Harrow (1977).

Krathwohl, Bloom, and Masia (1964) developed a taxonomy for the affective domain. Table 7.3 presents their major levels (or categories) from the least internalized to the most internalized. Also included are action verbs appropriate for each category.

The psychomotor domain originally was of interest to physical education teachers or early childhood teachers. Often it was used when dealing with fine- or gross-motor skills. Table 7.4 is an illustration of the taxonomy developed by Harrow (1977) for the psychomotor domain.

In viewing the verbs in each of the taxonomies, you will notice some overlapping within the various categories. In using the taxonomies, remember that the purpose is to formulate the best objectives for the job to be done. The taxonomies provide the mechanism for ensuring that you do not spend a disproportionate amount of time on simple recall of facts and low-order learning.

CONCLUSION

We might sum up this chapter by using an analogy. Kellough (1996) compares the head, heart, and hands to the cognitive, affective, and psychomotor domains. The cognitive domain is compared to the head because it involves mental processes. The affective domain is compared to the heart because it involves feelings and attitudes. The psychomotor domain is compared to the hands because it involves motor skills and manipulation.

REFERENCES

Bloom, B. S., Ed. 1984. *Taxonomy of educational objectives: Book I. Cognitive domain.* White Plains, N.Y.: Longman.

Harrow, A. J. 1977. *Taxonomy of the psychomotor domain.* White Plains, N.Y.: Longman.

Kellough, R. D. 1996a. *Integrating language arts and social studies for intermediate and middle school students.* Englewood Cliffs, N.J.: Merrill/Prentice Hall.

———. 1996b. *Integrating mathematics and science for intermediate and middle school students.* Englewood Cliffs, N.J.: Merrill/Prentice Hall.

Krathwohl, D. R., B. S. Bloom, and B. B. Masia. 1964. *Taxonomy of educational goals: Handbook II. Affective domain.* New York: McKay.

8

Display Your Assignments

This chapter addresses a very simple task that encompasses the areas of daily management, human relations/communications, planning, and your efforts to meet the needs of your students. This is a daily practice that successful educators use—writing in some form the assignments for the day. You may choose to use an overhead transparency, your chalkboard or whiteboard, or a notebook. This chapter is designed for teacher education candidates and also practicing teachers who are not utilizing this practice every day. If you are doing this each day in your classroom, please move to the last part of the chapter where some pearls of wisdom are given to enhance your management repertoire.

Obviously all teachers have written their plans in the lesson plan book (see chapter 6). This chapter addresses where and why to write the assignments elsewhere for the students' benefit.

When supervising first-year teachers, one of the things I look for is where or how teachers have posted their assignments for the students to view. Some prefer to write them on the chalkboard as they progress through their day. This approach, however, can cause confusion. For example, I have difficulty hearing the directions as the teacher has his or her head facing away from the class and is writing the assignment on the chalkboard or whiteboard. Other teachers prefer to write down every assignment before class begins in the morning. These teachers have moved from the role of teacher to that of professional. This method produces a smoother-running classroom—our optimum goal as a teacher.

One advantage of writing down assignments in advance is that the teacher doesn't need to check the lesson plan book and lose eye contact with the students while writing the assignment on the board. The flow of the classroom continues. With special needs students mainstreamed into the classrooms with problems from A to Z, it is good practice to make every effort to keep their attention rather than turning your back to the class to write those assignments on the chalkboard. Do it in advance.

A second advantage is also student focused. If a student leaves school early, everything is already written down. The student can copy down the assignments from the board before leaving. The teacher doesn't have to stop instruction to take care of this task. The responsibility is placed on the student.

Many schools require students to maintain an "assignment calendar." The students can easily write in the assignment if it is clearly written in view.

If a student is having trouble with organization (i.e., not turning in assignments), you can tell the parents that each assignment is written on the chalkboard or whiteboard every day—professionals are consistent. You are doing your part to provide the student with best-practice policies.

Finally, administrators, as well as any other individuals conducting your informal or formal observations/evaluations, will notice the assignments on the board. This is considered best practice among professionals.

I have seen middle school teachers use an entire chalkboard or a whiteboard to write down every assignment for the week. This is wonderful if a student is absent sometime during the week and returns by Friday. However, this approach is futile if the student returns on Monday. Think ahead!

Ask your principal whether it is required to write out assignments on the chalkboard or whiteboard each day. One school year I received some phone calls from irate teachers who taught at a site where the principal required *every* assignment to be written on the chalkboard *every* day. The kindergarten and first-grade teachers complained that the children couldn't even read yet! They felt that it was "busy work" for them and questioned the benefit of their labors. If your principal requires this, please comply graciously and cheerfully.

Aside from the requirement by the principal, why is it considered best practice to display your assignments each day? I go to schools in 100-degree weather and also in the dead of winter. Sometimes the window air conditioner units are working (hopefully), and sometimes the heaters are cranking. In either case, there is additional noise in the classroom. I generally sit at the back and often cannot hear directions or instructions clearly. Certainly the children sitting near the front can hear the teacher give a verbal explanation of the assignment or the page number, but not all students can hear clearly throughout the day. Thus, write it down for them and display it for all to see. Anyone with an attention problem, distractibility problem, or language or hearing problem can be directed to a specified site to read the assignment.

ADDITIONAL PEARLS OF WISDOM

Teachers with a limited amount of chalkboard or white board space can still write their assignments daily and post them. Most schools have a flipchart—a pad of large paper fastened together at the top and mounted on a stand or easel. Get out the flipchart and use it to display your assignments. If your school does not have a flipchart, you can request the school to purchase a Post-It brand pad designed by the 3M Company that measures twenty-five by thirty inches. (These pads can be purchased at most office supply stores.) Rather than purchase a stand or easel to hold the large pad, place it on the chalkboard tray when writing on it. This will save the district extra money and also save you classroom storage space. The sheets peel off and have the standard Post-It adhesive on the back so they will stick to the wall or over a window. You will create your own assignment sheet wherever you choose to place it. Because the sheets are so large, you can put several days of assignments on a single sheet. (Pearl of wisdom: If you can use these sheets to post assignments, just think of all the other great things you can do with them—*and* they will not damage the walls of the classroom!)

If your district will not purchase such a paper pad for you, all is not lost. Consider making one yourself. You can purchase a restickable glue stick at most multipurpose stores for $1.50 or less. If you use a standard glue stick, your paper will not release from the wall when you are finished with it. Therefore, seek out the restickable glue stick. Every school has large paper or large rolls of paper that you can tear to your specific length. Use this paper to write your assignments, and use the glue stick on the top of the underside. Your needs have been met with little effort or expense on your part.

Teachers concerned about using too much chalkboard or whiteboard space could use an assignment notebook. The notebook has the date and assignments written down each day, by either the teacher or a student helper. If a student is absent, he or she can use the notebook to write down the necessary assignments. Your assignment notebook can be a spiral-bound notebook purchased for less than $2 that will last the entire school year. Stick with something bound rather than individual file cards kept in a small box. These have the ability to "walk away" and become lost forever. Your goal is to keep everything *together*. Spend the money for a bound notebook of some sort, or create your own using a word processor and have it bound.

Another issue associated with the assignment notebook is where to keep it. One middle school teacher I observed had extra-large manila folders taped to the walls. He had a folder for every hour or period he taught. The folders were designed to hold makeup work. The students were responsible for putting their assignment into the appropriate folder. You could transpose this idea from holding makeup work to holding the assignment folder or folders. This would assist in organization and prevent the folders from "walking away." The folders could be labeled and hold an assignment notebook for every hour or period at the upper levels.

We have discussed nonprojected visuals up to this point. Now consider using projected visuals. Most classrooms have overhead projectors. If your projector has a "roller" system in which the film is rolled across the viewing area, you can write your assignments each day onto that film and show it to your classes. Some teachers use this system for an entire week, cleaning off the transparency film once a week. Keep a container of moistened sheets near the overhead machine for easy cleanup. Moistened sheets are sold at most grocery and pharmacy stores and are used for fast and simple cleanup. You could also use an overhead projector that uses single sheets of film for the same process. By using a Visa Vie pen (which is inexpensive and comes in an array of different colors), you can easily clean the transparency sheets after each use. One note: If you are planning to reuse the transparency film, be sure to use a nonpermanent marker. The permanent and nonpermanent markers are the same size and can be easily confused. The permanent markers cannot be erased from the transparency film.

A final suggestion for organizing and storing your daily assignments is to use a computer. If you have a large viewing monitor showing your computer screen, you could type out the assignments on the computer, and the text would be shown on the screen. Save your assignments for easy access.

CONCLUSION

Displaying your assignments each day is a sign of "best" teaching practice. You can maintain eye contact with the students, and the flow of the lesson is not deterred. If a student leaves in the middle of the day, the assignments are posted for easy copy. If you are using organizational tools, such as an assignment calendar, the students all have the advantage of viewing the assignments. Finally, your administrator and colleagues will see the assignments each day. It will reflect your abilities of management, human relations, planning, and sincere desire to best meet the needs of your students.

9

Substitute Folder

This chapter is designed for teachers in the field as well as the teacher education candidates. If you presently have a substitute folder, perhaps this chapter will give you suggestions and ideas to help you think outside the box in planning for the substitute.

Teacher education candidates can begin a "to do" list for their substitute folder after reading this chapter. This chapter will be helpful to cross-reference with the substitute folders you review in observations, internships, or clinical practice experiences—your fieldwork. When you are ready to set up your classroom, you will have all the components to create your own substitute folder.

Substitute teachers are wonderful people. They are versatile individuals who come into the lives of children for only a day or two at a time. Substitute teachers are not mind-readers; therefore, it is imperative for you to clearly state the specifics of your classroom.

Every classroom is special. Your students have special needs, both individually and collectively. Take time to put together a substitute folder that will withstand your school year. Tell the substitute specifically and in detail about the needs of your class. Do not, however, divulge confidential student information.

Save your information on a diskette. If you need to make a change sometime throughout the year (which always happens), you can simply go back and make a small change rather than retype the entire document.

Create a substitute folder with contents about your classroom. You might consider including some of the following suggestions:

- *A thank-you note.* How can you prepare a thank-you note in advance for a total stranger when you don't even know when you will be away from school? Easy! Write a generic thank-you letter. Show appreciation in advance for the substitute's efforts, time, talents, and compassion to your students. Include the thank-you letter at the beginning of your substitute folder. Thank this individual *in advance*, prior to his or her day in your shoes.
- *Your daily schedule.* Every teacher has a unique schedule. This will also be included with your lesson plans.
- *A map of the school.* Let the substitute see where the various rooms or buildings are located—especially the restrooms. Mark your classroom on the map just like you see the maps at the shopping malls marked with an X: "You are here."
- *Students with special schedules or pull-outs.* Do *not* write that Susan goes to learning disabilities class at 10:00 or that Joe goes to speech therapy at 9:00. Refer instead to the teacher's name rather than to the title of their job—for example, "Mrs. Jones's room" rather than "the Mentally Retarded classroom." Does the music teacher come to your room, or does the substitute walk the children to the music room? State the routine clearly. Take a few moments to be as specific as possible. Remember: Your substitute is a complete stranger to the site and to your classroom.
- *Names of students who take medication and the times of meds and where they are given.* For example: "Send Susan to the office at 11:00 to take medication." There is no need to specify the reason for the medication, such as for diabetes or ADD.
- *Disaster policy (fire, tornado, earthquake, etc.).* This information should be posted in the room close to the door for everyone to see at all times. Also put a copy in your substitute folder for convenience. By including and marking a school map, the substitute can see exactly where the students should be in case of a drill or disaster.
- *Your copying machine code number if available and/or necessary.* Many districts require a code number to use the copying machine. Without this number, the substitute cannot use the machine.

- *Instructions regarding a student with a specific medical condition.* For example, if a student is diabetic and has a snack at a certain time, write it down for the substitute. You might also obtain additional information in case of a medical emergency to add to your folder regarding this student. Cover every base so that every student can have a successful day at school.

- *Students who will be mainstreamed into your room and times.* Mainstreaming occurs in most schools in America. Children come and go throughout the day. Include the names of the students, the times they will be coming and going, and any additional specifics to make this transition easier for the child. Once again, the map that you have included will help the substitute to know where the child will be in proximity to the classroom. Does the teacher come to your room to pick up the student, or does the substitute dismiss the student at a specific time? State it clearly. Take a few moments to be as specific as possible. Again, your substitute is a complete stranger to the site and to your classroom.

- *What to do in case of inside recess.* Inside recess: a.k.a. the teacher's nightmare. Tell the substitute where you keep your puzzles, games, and other recess items. Specify anything that is considered "off limits" during inside recess. For example: Is the computer in your classroom to be used during inside recess?

- *Responsibilities of substitute regarding bathroom breaks, lunch breaks, recess, and so forth.* If the substitute is supposed to walk the students to the cafeteria before lunch, write it down. If the sub is supposed to meet the children at a designated door when recess is over, write it down with the specified time. Make these topics crystal-clear.

- *Any duties the substitute will be required to perform.* You may have recess duty on Wednesdays. You may have cafeteria duty on Tuesdays. Will the substitute need to eat lunch while walking around the cafeteria? You have bus duty on Thursday mornings. Where do you stand geographically on the school grounds, what time do you arrive, and what time do you leave your post? Explain the required time and location for the substitute. Once again, that map you included in the substitute folder will come in handy.

- *Specific instructions regarding a classroom computer(s).* If you wish the students to use the computer while you are gone, you will need to write down your password and any additional information necessary to get the computer up and running. You will also need to write down how to shut down the computer at the end of the day. Do not assign a student to start up and shut down the computer. It is the responsibility of an adult.

- *Class incentives.* Many teachers use some form of classroom incentive. If you allow the substitute to become part of this, you will need to include a detailed explanation of your incentive program. Don't leave the substitute in the dark on this one.

- *Anecdotal records.* You may wish for the substitute to leave you a written description of his or her day, detailing great or tragic experiences, and naming names. If this is your desire, please put your request in writing.

PLANNING

Most of us have heard the old saying "If you fail to plan, you plan to fail." In the teaching profession, this saying holds true. Part II has been about planning.

In all aspects of Part II, suggestions have been made to utilize technology. If technology can be used to create a custom designed lesson plan, what other ways can you use technology to save you time and energy? Technology is a vital aspect of the planning process. How can technology be used in the area of communications and human relations? How can technology assist you in student assessment? As you continue through the pages of this book, take time to think outside the box. Ask yourself "What if?" questions.

Technology is not our future—it is our present. If you are not proficient in technology, follow the steps in the Technology Excursions of this book to help you create documents that will be helpful to you and your students. Technology is one of those kinesthetic tasks—you learn by doing and you become better with practice. Embrace it and include it as part of your daily routine as a professional.

The best-practice suggestion here is to hone your tech skills and improve by daily use.

SUPPLY LIST

The final best-practice suggestion is to begin and organize a supply list for your classroom needs. Whether you are a teacher education candidate with a few semesters until you sign your teaching contract or a teacher in today's classroom, begin today keeping a list of supplies you will need for your classroom.

There is a major difference between what you "want" and what you "need." You may wish to start two different continuing lists. Include items you would love to have someday as well as necessary items. From a realistic perspective, the main focus of your list will be items you need to best educate your students, items to best help your students learn. Many suggestions for items appear in this book.

You may want to use a notebook to keep your list of items. Be sure you have easy access to that notebook. If you are a practicing teacher, consider using a page from your lesson plan book to jot down ideas for future classroom supplies. You might even add suggestions written on Post-It notes placed inside the cover of your grade book or lesson plan book. You decide on the location.

Many ideas in this book encourage you to think outside the box. Creative and innovative teachers will need some unique supplies to best complete this task. Consider technology supplies that will help you. Also consider the technology you have available or will have available at your school site.

Over time you will compile a great list of items. Organize them into the "needs" and "wants" categories. Also consider items that the students can bring at the beginning of the school year just as they bring pencils and paper. Some of the items on your list may be donations from parents, from a booster club or parent support organization at your school, or from a local business that sponsors your school. Revisit your list often to see how you can creatively obtain the items on our list in order to make your classroom a center for learning for all children.

III

THE ESSENTIALS OF PROFESSIONALISM: ASSESSMENT

Knowledge is learning something every day. Wisdom is letting go of something every day.

—Zen saying

After you have planned lessons to address student needs, you must assess. Suggestions are given for teachers using standard and technological grade books. Performance-based assessments are detailed with technology steps to create them yourself. Every teacher will benefit from the information on standardized testing. Descriptions of norm-referenced and criterion-referenced tests are given as well as the interpretations.

10

Grade Book

This chapter is intended for all three readerships. Teacher education candidates will benefit from general tips and accompanying visuals. Teachers in the field will learn specific tips, such as taking your backup disk or CD-RW home each night or how to set up the grade book to weigh grades. Feel free to check the subheadings for specific information. With all the information in this book, take the general information and tips and use them to meet your needs. Also consider them a springboard to assist you in thinking outside the box.

Grade books come in a variety of sizes and styles. Your district will supply you with a grade book. The format is generally the same: four sets of pages for subject A or hour 1, followed by four sets of pages for subject B or hour 2, and so on. The rationale for the four sets of pages corresponds with the four quarters of grading throughout the year.

The grade book is a vital tool. As with the lesson plan book, maintaining student grades will be a part of your overall evaluation. In Oklahoma, the lesson plan evaluation falls under the category of classroom management. As a university representative supervising first-year teachers, I look for ways in which the teacher "maintains a written record of student progress." I view the grade book for every subject or class period during every visit to the classroom as part of my evaluation.

PREPARATION

Many administrators will ask their teachers to use a special ledger sheet for the first two weeks of school. Students are dropping and adding classes at the beginning of school. Some districts use the third week of school as the bench-mark time to begin using the grade book.

Before beginning to write in the grade book, paper-clip the pages together so that you have the book divided into "hours" or subjects—three pages are clipped to the first page for each designated hour or subject. Three pages plus the first page equals a total of four pages per hour or subject.

When it is time to begin writing in the grade book, design it to flow with your daily routine. For example, hour 1 would come before hour 6. Self-contained classroom teachers or teachers with block scheduling would place the subjects in the order in which they are taught throughout the day. For example, a teacher working with a block style of schedule would first have "Section One: Math" followed by "Section One: Science" followed by Section Two and so forth.

SHORTCUT: WRITING NAMES IN THE GRADE BOOK

When you write your students' names in the grade book, consider leaving some space between groups of students. As the year progresses, you will have new students to add to the roster as well as students transferring out of your classes. By leaving some space between small groups of students, you can insert a new student in the approximate alphabet range where the name should be. I used to group my students by 4s or 5s and leave two or three spaces between groups. There is no set formula for the spacing of your students. Simply choose the formula that best meets your needs.

You have two choices when putting students' names in the grade book: either write them in by hand, or type them on a computer using a font size to fit the spacing of the grade book. Remember to save the names on a disk. Consider writing down (or typing) four or five names, leave some space, and write down four or five more spaces, and so on. The spaces will be filled in throughout the year as new students enroll in your school. If you are a self-contained classroom teacher or a teacher with block scheduling (having the same students for more than one class), take the first page to the photocopying machine and make copies. Cut and paste the copied names onto the first page of your next section. Rubber cement or a glue stick will keep the paper flat and smooth. A permanent glue stick, rather than a restickable glue stick, works best for this project. (Liquid glue often wrinkles the paper.) Save time—cut and paste.

AFTER THE FIRST QUARTER

After the first quarter, move to the second page of your four-page section. Some grade books allow the teacher to fold back a section for the names to show for all four quarters. If your grade book does not have this feature, photocopy the names from the first page and cut and paste them to this one. Adjust the paper clip, and you are ready to begin a new quarter.

POTENTIAL PROBLEM: NOT ENOUGH LINES

Some districts purchase manufactured grade books that do not have enough lines to list all the students in one class. The teachers have too many students to fit their names on the same page of the grade book. This is not the fault of the teacher but the district that bought identical grade books for *every* teacher in the district. Some teachers have more than twenty students per class, yet only twenty spaces in the grade book.

Your choices include the following:

1. Request a grade book that has enough spaces for your needs,
2. Purchase a grade book that has enough spaces for your needs, or
3. Design your own with the approval of your administrator.

Take it to the local photocopy shop for printing and a spiral binding. Be sure that the binding allows the book to lay flat and also fold easily. Take the time to make your building administrator aware of your problem. In all likelihood, you are not the only individual at your site or in your district with this problem. If your district cannot assist you this year, the administration will likely try to meet your need for the next year. Please make your administrator aware of the problem.

TIME-SAVING TIP TO CALCULATE GRADES

Many districts do not provide computers and grading programs for teachers. Many teachers do not choose to use computerized grading programs. If you are maintaining your grades manually, either by choice or by necessity, consider the following tip. Average your grades every Friday or on the weekend for that particular week's assignments. You will have five or fewer scores to average. Write the average in a different color of ink to help you differentiate between the daily scores and the *average* for the week. Figure 10.1 shows one

FIGURE 10.1
One week's grades with average

84	80	96	88	88.5

week in the grade book and the week's average. (Rather than using two different colors of ink, I have used two different font sizes for this illustration.)

When progress reports come around, you will only have four grades to average per student as opposed to ten to twenty grades per student. When grade cards are due, you will only have nine grades (the weekly averages) to add up and find the average.

WEIGHING GRADES

Some teachers "weigh" grades. They put more weight on a specific grade, such as a test or project, compared to a daily grade. Figure 10.2 is a grade book that shows a test grade multiplied or "weighted" three times. The smaller numbers above the grades indicate the total number of points for each assignment.

Some teachers choose not to give each assignment a hundred-point value. This is very common in primary elementary classes when only three or four questions are completed by students. In this case, teachers may choose to work with a "total point" system in which they write the total points possible above the grades in the grade book. They then insert the students' grades below. Figure 10.3 is a sample grade book that shows total points possible rather than a hundred-point value for every assignment.

If you choose to use a computerized grading program, check out all the parameters of the program before you decide to weigh grades. The program you use may not have the capability to weigh grades. You therefore will only have the choice of a hundred-point value for each assignment. If you wish for your tests to count for a greater value, just insert them to equal that amount. The

FIGURE 10.2
Weighed grades with daily grades

100	100	300	100	100
82	90	285	85	94

FIGURE 10.3
Total possible points with average

	18	24	15	12	20	9	98 Total Points	Percentage
Beth Bonner	16	24	14	10	18	7	89	90.8
Guy Green	18	22	12	11	15	5	83	84.7
Samantha Smith	15	20	14	12	19	7	87	88.8

FIGURE 10.4
Daily grades with weighed test grades

	Page 47	Qu 1–12	Pg 51–52	Test	Test	Test	Page 55	Qu 7–17	Percentage
Beth Bonner	100	98	89	95	95	95	77	82	92.5
Guy Green	98	72	61	90	90	90	79	100	85
Samantha Smith	82	87	100	85	85	85	100	100	90.5

sample in figure 10.4 shows both daily grades of a hundred-point value and a test worth three hundred points.

MAINTAINING THE GRADE BOOK

Many teachers have the opportunity to maintain student records (grades) on a computer. If this is your choice, I strongly advise that you maintain the grades on the computer (with a disk or CD-R backup) as well as in written form in a grade book. (Remember the difference between CDs. You want the one that allows you to rewrite to it. It is more expensive, but one CD will allow you to store students' grades for years. CDs have huge memory capacity when compared to disks. If you purchase a CD-R, you cannot continue to rewrite to it. Yes, it is less expensive, but it will not meet your needs.) Your evaluators will prefer viewing the tangible grade book rather than starting up a computer and searching for specific grades during an evaluation session.

Several districts provide computers and grading programs to faculty members. Many districtwide grading programs also allow the teacher to print out grade cards and progress reports. This is a major time saver, compared to the old manual system of writing everything out using multicarbon sheets.

Please remember to keep the grade book shut while at school, unless in current use. A closed grade book promotes and maintains student confidentiality.

If you are maintaining grades using a computer, do not enter grades during class time or in front of students or parents. Individuals can view the screen and learn confidential information on other students.

Also, consider taking your backup disk or CD-RW home with you each evening. This is extra insurance that if damage or theft occurs at the school overnight, you are still covered with your backup information. Many districts require the teacher to carry the grade book out of the school during fire drills or other disaster drills. If you are using a computer to maintain your grades, take out your backup disk or CD-RW during the drill. Obviously, you cannot disconnect and carry out a large computer!

Aside from the obvious advantages of using a computer program to store your grades, the teacher can instantly see student averages throughout the grading period. In a district with high mobility of students, this would be particularly helpful when a student suddenly moves away. The teacher can have student records instantly. I used a program that allowed me to print out the mean or average of each student and subject for progress reports. I no longer spent hours laboring over a calculator every few weeks.

ADDITIONAL INFORMATION

Some districts require the teacher to keep additional information as well as records in the grade book. The following list suggests some information to keep in the grade book other than grades:

- Often teachers record the number of the textbook in the first space beside the student's name. This can easily be checked at the end of the school year or when the student transfers to another school.
- Some teachers also write the student's locker number and/or locker combination in the grade book beside the name.
- Some administrators require that the teacher keep a record of attendance. That information can easily be maintained in the grade book.
- Some teachers keep a record of the student's birthday in the grade book. Everyone, no matter what age or grade, enjoys being recognized on his or her birthday.

• You might also wish to write the bus number on which the student travels or a phone number to contact during daytime hours.

CONCLUSION

Grade books, just like lesson plans, are a daily task for teachers. This chapter has given information regarding preparation, writing names in the grade book, time-saving tips to calculating grades, the topic of weighing grades, and general tips on maintaining grades. Your grade book will be a vital tool to you during formative assessments on a daily basis, as well as during progress report or grade card time. Your grade book will also be viewed by your administrator and others during your evaluation process.

WEB REFERENCES

www.experttesting.com. Site for Expert Grader.

www.1st-class-software.com. Site for 1st Class Grade book.

www.gradebook.com. Site for Grade book software.

www.mistycity.com. Site for Grade Machine.

www.jacksoncorp.com/gradequick. Site for Grade Quick.

www.shelltech.com/. Site for Grade Star.

Reporting Students' Progress

The purpose of this chapter is to supply the teacher with unique strategies to report student progress. Many districts require teachers to compile and send home a standard progress report. This chapter moves away from the standard form and gives the teacher ideas on receiving feedback, establishing short-term student goals, and best achieving the concept of reporting student progress. Ideas in this chapter will assist you to "work smart" in order to use the least amount of time to achieve the maximum results. If you are a teacher education candidate or an alternative certification teacher, please read the entire chapter. The information will be helpful and enlightening to you. If you are a practicing teacher, please move on to the latter part of the chapter for creative and unique ideas.

As a classroom teacher, you will be communicating your students' progress many times throughout the school year. Whether your district is divided into four quarters or three trimesters, you will be required to prepare grade cards. Prior to grade card time, you will also have a midpoint in which you will prepare a "progress report." Grade cards are mandatory for every student. Your district may or may not require every student to receive a progress report.

Take a mathematical approach to the responsibility to communicating students' grades. If you teach at the elementary level, you probably have six core curricular subjects in which you are maintaining grades for every child. If you have a class of twenty students, that is 20 times 6 sets of grades to average and prepare each reporting session. Although you only have 20 sets of reports, you have to record 120 grades. If you are a secondary teacher teaching 6 sections with 20 students in each class, you have the same number of grades but rather than only having 20 papers to prepare, you will have 120—same work but more paperwork.

Taking these data, look at the numbers over the course of an entire school year. Calculate 120 grades multiplied by 4 for the 4 quarters in a school year. The result is 480 grades for the school year. A true professional would surely send every student a progress report also. The calculation for that would be 480 grades multiplied by 2, or 960 total grades calculated each school year.

In the previous chapter, both the traditional grade book and the computerized grade book were discussed. Advantages for both were viewed. I have been in the profession long enough to see the progression from feeling as if the calculator might become a permanent body part to seeing the value of technology. Consider the options that you have available. Consider also the mathematical calculations of the high number of grades you will be required to maintain and tabulate.

ADDITIONAL PEARLS OF WISDOM

When progress report time comes around, consider sending home an accompanying form for the parents and student to complete and return to you. The question format can be in one of two designs. The *select format* allows the individual *to select* the answer from a given number of alternatives. The *supply format* allows the individual to write in or supply responses. (The concept of supply/select formats stems from tests and measurements courses. Students learn how to construct supply questions such as essay or short-answer questions. They also learn how to write select questions, such as multiple-choice, true/false, or matching questions. This concept is just made into a workable form for this purpose.) Either way, the classroom teacher will receive special feedback regarding every student. The student and parent can discuss the progress report and set a goal or goals for the remaining period of time before grade cards are reported.

Table 11.1 is a sample of a checklist (select format) for parents and students to complete and return. Table 11.2 is a free response or supply format example.

Table 11.1.   Select Format

XYZ Public Schools

Enclosed you will find a progress report showing grades since the last grade card was recorded. Could you please review the grades and then complete and return the following information? We may then generate a course of action that may help the student maintain his or her present standing or improve within the next four weeks. Thank you for your assistance.

Please write additional comments on the back of this form.

Jane Doe

Student Response	Parent Response
Give your response to the progress report ____Very satisfied ____See areas in which I can improve ____Dissatisfied with the report	Give your response to the progress report ____Very satisfied ____See areas in which my child can improve ____Dissatisfied with the report
I would rate my level of effort as: ____My best ability ____I worked hard most of the time ____I rarely worked to my ability	I would rate my child's level of effort as: ____The best ability ____He/she worked hard most of the time ____He/she rarely worked to the best ability
If I want to improve, I should ____Complete every assignment ____Turn in every assignment on time ____Study better for tests ____Participate better in class ____Improve my organization skills ____Bring home communications and books ____Improve my listening skills ____Bring my supplies to class	If my child wants to improve, he/she should ____Complete every assignment ____Turn in every assignment on time ____Study better for tests ____Participate better in class ____Improve organization skills ____Bring home communications and books ____Improve listening skills ____Bring supplies to class
Student signature _____	Parent signature _____

You can utilize this information to design a strategy to best help the student during the next four weeks—the time frame till grade cards are tabulated. The information that you harvest from these forms or a similar one that you prepare will be invaluable to you as a professional. For example, if a student is not performing well on simple basic addition and subtraction facts and you learn that he or she is using flash cards at home every night, perhaps some type of learning problem is affecting the child's progress. On the flip side of that scenario, if a child is not performing well on simple basic addition and subtraction facts and

Table 11.2. Supply Format

XYZ Public Schools

Enclosed you will find a progress report showing grades since the last grade card was recorded. Could you please review the grades and then complete and return the following information? We may then generate a course of action that may help the student maintain his or her present standing or improve within the next four weeks. Thank you for your assistance.

Jane Doe

Student Response	Parent Response
Describe your response to your progress report.	Describe your response to your child's progress report.
Describe your level of effort for this grading period.	Describe your child's level of effort for this grading period.
List ways in which you can improve your grades over the next four weeks.	List ways in which your child can improve his/her grades over the next four weeks.
Personal goal: Over the next four weeks I will do my very best to:	Parental goal: Over the next four weeks we will work at home on:
Student signature _____	Parent signature _____

you learn that no efforts are being made at home to help, you can send home flash cards and see whether the student improves with the extra assistance.

You can also use this as a follow-up or postassessment when grade cards are given to students. Did their efforts return high dividends for them? Did the students realize that they had areas in which they could improve?

This information will also be helpful as a tool to use when parents come for conferences. You will have the copy to show them their responses and discuss how the partnership between home and school helped to benefit the student. This data can be used in many ways during conferences.

If teachers in your district are required to maintain a professional portfolio or prepare an end of the year report, the form you prepared and a short description of advantages would be an admirable addition. Also showing this form in a job interview for a future job would be highly impressive to the interview committee. A final advantage for custom-designing a form for parental and student feedback is that your administrator will be able to see documentation that you have made a sincere effort to communicate with parents and students. It is a wonderful display of human relations skills.

Check with your administrator about specifically how grades and progress reports are to be presented to the students and parents. If you design your own progress report form, you might consider custom-tailoring your form to meet your specific needs. For example, a technology teacher would have specific skills that are required for mastery that other teachers may not include, such as keyboard typing and flowchart design. A physical education teacher, visual arts teacher, or music teacher would have performance objectives much different from a classroom teacher teaching core curricular areas. At the secondary level, a science teacher who includes a lab as part of the course might include laboratory objectives along with content objectives. Obviously the science teacher's objectives would vary from those of the English teacher or foreign language teacher.

When I was a sixth-grade self-contained classroom teacher, the progress report forms were used for all elementary students from first through sixth grades. There was a space to check if my students could count in written form or orally from one to twenty-five or from one to one hundred. I wanted to add a space for "uses the value of pi to calculate the area of a circle." My administrator graciously allowed me to design a form that would be appropriate for sixth graders and our sixth-grade objectives. I was the first member of her faculty that had ever made such a request.

According to Linn and Gronlund (2000: 381), "to provide more informative progress reports, some schools have replaced or supplemented the traditional grading system with a list of objectives to be checked or rated." More information is given in each subject area than just "Math—A." The following is an example of a supplement that might accompany a mathematics grade:

Arithmetic
1. Uses fundamental processes
2. Solves problems involving reasoning
3. Is accurate in work
4. Works at a satisfactory rate

Perhaps you might choose to add some additional information, which might in some way affect the child's progress. Please see the following example:

Arithmetic
1. Uses fundamental processes
2. Solves problems involving reasoning
3. Is accurate in work
4. Works at a satisfactory rate
5. Works without distractions
6. Completes assignments
7. Turns in assignments on time

Linn and Gronlund (2000) further elaborate that the checklist as a form of reporting has the obvious advantage of

> providing a detailed analysis of the student's strengths and weaknesses so that constructive action can be taken to help improve learning. It also provides students, parents, and others with a frequent reminder of the school's objectives. The main difficulties encountered with such reports are in keeping the list of statements down to a workable number and in stating them in such simple and concise terms that they are readily understood by all users of the reports. (384)

This form of reporting would be extremely helpful to use with preschool or primary students who perhaps do not receive a letter grade.

Aside from establishing your "indicators," the symbols used to rate students on each of the major objectives vary considerably. In some districts, the standard A, B, C, D, and F remain. As a teacher in a district with high student movement, I often struggled to find out exactly what an "A" actually was. Did the district use the "ten-point rule" of A = 90–100, B = 90–89, and so forth? Or did the district use the "seven-point rule" in which A = 100–93, B = 92–85, and so on? If this new student coming in from another district was a "straight A" student, what did that actually mean? I continue to struggle with the "minus" and "plus" attached to letter grades. Those symbols are vague. Rarely are criteria written down for future teachers in other districts to decipher. Therefore, my favorite way of reporting grades for parents, teachers, future teachers, and students is the number grade that has the least margin for debate. A 90 percent is a 90 percent is a 90 percent.

CONCLUSION

As a classroom teacher you will be required to calculate students' grades at progress report time, grade card time, when a student moves away, and perhaps when preparing documentation for a student to be tested for special services. As a professional, consider designing a form that will best inform parents and students of the progress that has been made. When sending home a progress report, try constructing a set of supply or select questions to go home with the report. The feedback from the students and parents will be valuable to you throughout the remainder of the school year.

REFERENCE

Linn, R. L., and N. E. Gronlund. 2000. *Measurement and assessment in teaching.* 8th ed. Upper Saddle River, N.J.: Merrill/Prentice Hall.

Evaluation of Students

The evaluation process of students truly spans the spectrum. As educators, our tasks range from attempting to evaluate the strengths and weaknesses of a four-year-old who cannot read or write to evaluating a high school senior taking advanced placement classes—and every student and every curricular area in between. The evaluation tools stretch from the traditional paper-and-pencil tests that we recall from our days as a student to authentic assessment instruments. This chapter will provide you with an overview of the student evaluation process. Alternative certification candidates and teacher education candidates will benefit from the contents of the entire chapter.

Classroom testing, assessment, or evaluation "is to obtain valid, reliable, and useful information concerning student achievement" (Linn and Gronlund 2000: 139). The term *validity*, as used in testing and assessment, refers to the interpretation of the results. In laymen's terms, validity asks the question "Does it do (or measure) what it says it will do (or measure)?" *Reliability* is synonymous with *consistency*. Are the results consistent?

Consider the following steps regarding assessment:

- Determine the purpose of measurement. Is it formative? Summative? Pretest? Posttest? Why are the students taking this assessment instrument?
- What type of test format will best evaluate the objectives? If you have conducted laboratory experiments, will you have performance-based assessments or stay with the traditional paper-and-pencil test? If your students

have lower-level writing abilities, use a method other than the essay format. Select a format that will be best for the students, rather than easiest for you to grade. Professionals are student focused.

- Assemble the assessment with the focus on your objectives throughout the unit. All supplementary materials, assignments, readings, visual aids, videos, and so forth have centered on the teaching objectives. The objectives for the unit must also be the heart of the test questions.

- Administer the assessment. Allow plenty of time for the students to complete the assessment. Provide a quiet and comfortable testing climate. Discuss prior to the test what the students are to do when they complete the test. Monitor the students while they are being tested. It may be necessary for you to rearrange the seating to provide for a more secure testing environment. If your desks are in "quads" or grouped, consider rearranging them in the traditional rows for the test.

- Evaluate the assessment. See "Student Confidentiality" (chapter 19) for further information. The teacher will grade the tests, record the tests, and pass the tests back to the students.

- Reflect on the evaluation results as well as on the assessment results. What changes can be made to best assess every student next time? What teaching strategies need to be included or omitted to best facilitate learning?

- Record the results. Use your grade book or electronic grading program to record the results. You may want to "weigh" the assessment—multiply this score by two, three, or whatever, so the value will be greater than that of a daily grade.

- Analyze and reflect on the results both collectively and individually in order to improve learning and instruction.

ASSESSMENT BEFORE, DURING, AND AFTER

Many educators use a pretest for diagnostic purposes. Elementary teachers will often give a spelling pretest at the beginning of the week, followed by a posttest on Friday. The students know the words they need to study for the week. Linn and Gronlund (2000) suggest that pretests should be used to determine readiness or to determine student placement.

Readiness pretests are used to test entire classes at the beginning of the school year. These pretests can be administered in any curricular area. Pretests help the teacher create a road map of the students' strengths and weaknesses.

Often the teacher will decide to begin with chapter 2 or 3 based on class pretest results. Pretests are often also administered when a new student arrives during the school year. Therefore, pretests can be administered individually or in a group setting for any curricular subject at any time throughout the year.

One cautionary thought to consider when using readiness pretests is to look carefully at your assessment instrument. If students have completed the third grade in May and enrolled in the fourth grade in August, do not give them an end-of-the-year fourth-grade-level test. Use, instead, an end-of-the-year third grade assessment. This situation arose at a school one year when every student with low mathematics scores was tested for remedial mathematics. They were given the end-of-the-year mathematics test in the fall for the grade level that they were enrolled in that year. Finally, someone discovered that they should have been given the end-of-the-year test at the previous grade level. Look carefully at your pretest and also your purpose for testing.

Formative assessment includes your daily assignments, quizzes, or practice tests. It provides the teacher with information about specific objectives and daily instruction. If the entire class is struggling with a specific concept, rearrange your lesson plans to allow for reteaching lessons. Formative assessment allows the teacher to detect a systematic error made by a few students. Students make systematic errors in virtually every curricular discipline and at all levels. When papers are corrected as soon as possible, the teacher is aware of the problem instantly. By working individually with the student to correct this systematic error, the student can then move on and master that skill.

An example of a systematic error in mathematics is when the same mistake is made systematically—over and over again. Regrouping in addition and subtraction (the old borrowing and carrying from our days as a student) is often a systematic error.

Note the systematic errors made in "carrying" or regrouping in addition here:

$$\begin{array}{r} 17 \\ + 18 \\ \hline 215 \end{array} \qquad \begin{array}{l} 7 + 8 = 15 \\ \underline{1 + 1} = 2 \end{array}$$

The student's answer is 215 rather than 35.

A second display of a systematic error is the following:

26          $6 + 4 = 10$

+ 14

310         $2 + 1 = 3 + 10 = 310$ rather than 40

Here are two examples of systematic errors made in the "borrowing" phase of subtraction:

61          $7 - 1 = 6$

− 7   Bring down 6 from 10's column.

66   Answer is 66 rather than 54.

71          $9 - 1 = 8$

− 9   Bring down 7 from 10's column.

78   Answer is 78 rather than 62.

Systematic errors can be corrected quickly by staying current on grading student papers and also by working independently with the student to help him or her understand the reason for the error. If the teacher waits several days after an assignment to grade daily work, the systematic errors have occurred over a long-term time span rather than just one day.

Formative assessment can also include verbally questioning the class throughout the lesson to see whether the students are grasping the lesson objectives. If not, review the concept again or change instruction to assist the students. As a university representative, I have seen the well-prepared first-year teacher teach a lesson in which the students just didn't grasp the concept. When he or she finally realized that things were just not working, they tried a plan B—used the chalkboard for an illustration, brought out manipulatives, used overhead transparencies for visual assistance, or used models such as a globe—any trick from their repertoire to promote student learning.

Summative assessment is the "grand finale." Chapter tests, cumulative end-of-the-quarter tests or cumulative semester tests, and posttests are examples of summative evaluations. Summative tests are a summation of learned information and content over a specified amount of material. In college you took midterm and semester tests. They were a summation of the information covered up to that point. In American classrooms today, summative tests are given in school just before the teacher packs up the unit or chapter and puts it away in the file cabinet. The test is a summation of that information. The teacher will not get that folder out again until next year.

OBJECTIVE/PERFORMANCE TESTS

Objective tests require the student to supply or select one single correct answer. In a supply format, the student supplies or gives the answer. An example of a supply question would be a fill-in-the-blank or short-answer question. In a select format the student selects from several choices the one he or she believes to be correct. An example of a select question would be a multiple-choice, true/false, or matching question.

In all cases, there is just a single answer that is correct. These are referred to as *convergent* questions—lower-level, basic recall questions. An example of a convergent question could be "Who was the first female to receive the Nobel Prize?" Objective test questions are very easy for the teacher to correct, because there is no margin of error or area to debate.

Performance tests are subjective in nature. Essay tests allow the student to organize and write responses. Performance classes such as music or speech allow students to sing, play, or give a speech in front of an audience as part of their assessment. Classes such as agriculture, technology, family living, or science allow the student to utilize certain equipment as part of their assessment. Other subject areas such as music or foreign language require the student to perform a task that is judged subjectively by the teacher.

Performance tests are difficult for the teacher to assess. There is also much room for debate between the student and the teacher when performance tests are used. Performance essay questions can be *divergent* questions with several correct answers. Divergent questions are higher-order thinking questions that utilize the upper realm of Bloom's taxonomy, such as analysis or evaluation.

Divergent questions are wonderful opportunities for whole-group or small-group discussions. When working with divergent questions for the first time, some students couldn't understand why their answer was different from someone else's answer and *both* were considered correct. As a classroom teacher, you can introduce divergent questions with any age group or ability level.

Here are some examples of divergent questions:

- Why did Europeans come to the New World?
- In which biome or habitat did Laura Ingalls's family live?
- What is your favorite topping on a pizza?
- What was the main goal in the race into space between the United States and the USSR?
- Why should the depletion of the rain forest be stopped?

CONCLUSION

The evaluation of students comes in many forms. Just as lesson planning involves much decision making on the part of the teacher, so does the evaluation process. Always tie the assessment questions back to the daily teaching objectives (those measurable verbs from chapter 7). Assessment of students is part of being an educator. Our assessment designs and methods of maintaining those results become part of our evaluation process.

This chapter directly ties to the major topics of this book. Student assessment connects to addressing student needs, planning, assessment, and communications and human relations. If student evaluation results are poor, each topic needs to be revisited.

REFERENCES

Airasian, P. 1997. *Classroom assessment.* 3d ed. New York: McGraw-Hill.

Linn, R. L., and N. E. Gronlund. 2000. *Measurement and assessment in teaching.* 8th ed. Upper Saddle River, N.J.: Merrill/Prentice Hall.

Checklists, Rating Scales, and Rubrics

When teaching strategies allow students to produce or perform, performance-based assessments are required. Rubrics, checklists, and rating scales all have specific purposes. One cannot be easily interchanged for the other. This chapter focuses on the purpose and design of these three assessments.

Teacher education candidates will be able to read this chapter and create the various performance-based assessments using a personal computer or one at the university computer lab. This information will be helpful when creating lesson plans, teaching units, or preparing for courses such as tests and measurements or measurements and evaluations. The teachers in the field can read this information and create performance-based assessments for use with students in classes tomorrow or later in the week. Save your work on a diskette or on the computer hard drive. It will serve as useful samples for teacher education candidates' portfolios or a professional portfolio or end-of-the-year report for the practicing teacher.

𝕵 Teachers today have technology available in which they can create performance-based assessments. They can also save the instrument and then easily adapt it for future use. The examples provided in this chapter were created using Microsoft Word and its "Table" feature. These examples do not take up an entire page due to efforts to save space. As a classroom teacher, you could create larger assessment tools that do use an 8½ by 11-inch sheet of paper. As you read this chapter, look for the Technology Excursion Trip information. This will assist you in creating checklists, rating scales, and rubrics.

Throughout this chapter you will see examples in which the teacher, students, and a peer may conduct an evaluation. Obviously the teacher should be part of the evaluation process. Self-assessment is a great way to get students to go back and critically view and reflect on their work. As a classroom teacher, I always wanted my students to double-check their work before hastily turning it in for evaluation. A self-assessment tool is a solution to that problem. The student can use the evaluation tool to seriously view his or her own strengths and weaknesses.

Do not be concerned about violating student confidentiality when using peer evaluations. By using a performance-based assessment instrument, a fellow student can examine another student's work without ever seeing how the teacher evaluated the work. Examples of the assessment instrument are included in this chapter. You can even set up the peer evaluation in which the peer evaluates a "blind" paper—one without a name on it so that the peer does not know the identity of the author. The peer gets to compare his or her work against another model and both see and learn from other works. As Abraham Maslow said, "We learn from the experiences of others." In this case, the peers are learning from the efforts of others.

Peer reviews are not intended to become a popularity contest or pupil opinion. Instead, they allow the peer to use the same criteria in which he or she is evaluated. Peer reviews are intended to be a learning process for everyone.

Performance-based assessments have many benefits to the teacher and student, which will be discussed later, but they also have some potential errors associated with them:

- Because they are considered subjective in nature, there can be room for debate and discussion by the student and also the parent. Make every effort to be fair and consistent.
- The teacher can be accused of being biased. Remember the old "personality conflict" issue that we hear about at school between a teacher and a student? This topic can arise when using subjective grading. Whether it be a personality conflict or gender, cultural, racial, or religious issue, teachers can be accused of being biased in grading. If you give the scoring rubric to the students in advance, you have made every effort for every student to know the scoring criteria.

- Be as objective as possible. Avoid the "Santa Claus" syndrome. Too often the teacher will give *everyone* high scores. When I am grading teaching units completed by my university students, I try to read through every one *prior* to grading them. I will then have some idea of the level of work. I then try to grade all the units in one sitting to ensure fairness.
- Two other potential pitfalls are giving *everyone* a "middle of the road" grade (average) or a less-than-average grade (the "Grinch" syndrome"). Make every effort to recognize the strengths and weaknesses within each body of work.

CHECKLISTS

Checklists are the simplest assessment tool to analyze. A checklist consists of a set of written criteria. The teacher simply checks yes or no as to whether the student has achieved the criteria. With some checklists, the teacher simply makes a check mark if the criteria are achieved. Often a checklist is used in correspondence with a portfolio (see the next chapter). The student is required to put specific things inside the portfolio, and the teacher checks the contents.

Checklists are diagnostic, reusable, and capable of charting pupil progress as well as strengths and weaknesses. They provide a detailed record of performances, one that can and should be shown to pupils to help them see where improvement is needed (Airasian 1997). Checklists offer feedback to the student and also can be used during parent–teacher conferences to discuss the student's progress.

There are, however, some disadvantages to using a checklists. The teacher has only two choices during the evaluation process—the criteria was or was not achieved. The teacher must decide absolutely yes or no. Too often the student's performance is somewhere in between. A second disadvantage arises when the teacher is looking beyond strengths and weaknesses. A checklist does not give a total composite of the student's abilities.

Primary or preschool teachers often use checklists to record whether the student has achieved specific goals, such as "counts from one to ten orally." A checklist can also show the date when the student achieves the goal. Table 13.1 is a sample of a checklist for a mathematics student.

Checklists can coincide with a portfolio. The checklist easily displays what is inside or not inside the portfolio. Table 13.2 is a checklist illustrating the contents of a student portfolio. Note that this checklist has a provision for the teacher, the peer, and the student to check the contents.

Table 13.1.   Addition and Subtraction Student Checklist

Student's name_____

✓ Student can add two- and three-digit numbers without regrouping.
✓ Student can add two-digit numbers with regrouping.
  Student can add three-digit numbers with regrouping.
✓ Student can subtract two- and three-digit numbers without regrouping.
  Student can subtract two-digit numbers with regrouping.
  Student can subtract three-digit numbers with regrouping.
✓ Student can add dollars and cents up to $9.99.
  Student can subtract dollars and cents up to $9.99.
✓ Student can add ones and tenths.
  Student can subtract ones and tenths.

Comments:

✦ **Technology Excursion Trip**   *This checklist was created by opening Word, going to Table, then Insert. I used One Row, One Column. I adjusted the height of my rows to fit the content I wished to use.*

The checkmarks are set up as Bullets. Go to Format, then Bullets and Numbering. You will have a myriad of choices from which to select. I selected a check mark, because this is a checklist.

You can create checklists, rating scales, and rubrics for your class assignments. Remember to always do two things:

1. *Always give the students the grading assessment tool before they begin the assignment. They return it to you with the assignment. They have had it at home when they worked on and completed the work. Often students will write positive comments about this practice on evaluations.*
2. *Always put a row at the bottom of your assessment for comments. The comments can be made by the teacher or the student. If you create a rubric or checklist and forget to leave a row for comments, just highlight the bottom row, go back to Table, then to Insert, Row at Bottom. Presto, chango—you will now have a row for comments at the bottom of your assessment tool.*

RATING SCALES

While checklists give only two choices for each criterion, rating scales provide a more detailed diagnosis of the student's performance. Checklists look at the yes or no aspect of a criteria. Rating scales look at the performance judges in terms of *degree*, rather than the presence or absence of criteria. Rating scales are used with several degrees of proficiency, such as *excellent, good, fair, poor* or *sometimes, rarely,* or *never.*

Table 13.2.   Teacher-Student-Peer Checklist for Portfolio

Portfolio Checklist

Student's name _____

Date _____

Teacher Date _____ Signature _____

Student Date _____ Signature _____

Peer Date _____ Signature _____

Choices	*Requirements*
____choose favorite mathematics paper ____choose favorite language arts paper ____choose favorite social studies paper ____choose favorite science paper ____choose favorite project COMMENTS:	____1 mathematics assignment ____1 language arts assignment ____1 social studies assignment ____1 science assignment ____project from any area

✦ **Technology Excursion Trip**   *This checklist was created using the same steps as previously mentioned. However, I used Two Rows and One Column. Highlight the bottom row, and then go to Table again and select Split Cells. Select two columns rather than one. That will give you two columns on the bottom row and only one on the top. You can also merge cells by highlighting them and going to Table, Merge Cells. If you ever make mistakes when working with tables (which is often the case), remember to use the back arrow on your toolbar for assistance. That arrow will return the information you had prior to your most recent selection.*

With numerical rating scales, a number value is assigned to each description or indicator so that the teacher can assign a numerical value for the assignment, project, or task. "Numerical summarization is the most straightforward and commonly used approach to summarizing performance on rating scales. It assigns a point value to each category in the scale and sums the points across the performance criteria" (Airasian 1997: 231).

Rating scales are useful with all performance-based activities. They focus on the same aspects for every student. There are benefits for both the teacher and student regarding rating scales. If the rating scale has been prepared in terms of specific learning outcomes, it also serves as an excellent teaching device. The dimensions and behavior descriptions used in the scale show the student the type of performance desired (Linn and Gronlund 2000: 275).

Rating scales can also be used to show progress as well as the end or finished "product." The behavior chart examples (see chapter 21) show a student's behaviors for the week or for the month. This is an example of the progress the student is making in specific areas. Rating scales can also be used to show progress in musical performance, art, technology, family living skills, drafting, woodworking, or any performance-based course.

Several different types of rating scales are possible. The three most common are the numerical, the graphic, and the descriptive rating scale. The numerical rating scale allows the teacher to assign a number value, thus utilizing this form to assign grades. The graphic and descriptive rating scales provide students with detailed information regarding their performance-based task.

Airasian (1997) suggests two rules to consider when using rating scales with your students. First, limit the number of rating categories. Small numbers are much easier and more efficient to manage. Second, strive to use the same rating scale for each performance criterion. The descriptive scale changes with each assignment. However, "for the numerical and graphic scales it is best to select a single rating scale and use it for all performance criteria" (Airasian 1997: 228). The student will benefit from using the same criteria each time he or she is evaluated. The teacher will know the criteria well when using the same evaluation instrument each time. This will reduce distractions and save time.

Table 13.3 is an example of a numerical rating scale. Please note the space at the bottom for comments from the evaluator. As with all performance-based evaluations, I recommend that a place be provided for the teacher's positive and constructive comments for the students.

The next example (table 13.4) is the previous information transformed into a descriptive rating scale. "Descriptions" are used to determine or rate the student's progress.

A modification of the descriptive rating scale would be to use symbols—or graphics—rather than words as descriptors. Table 13.5 presents the same information transposed into a symbolic system of reporting the student's progress—a graphic rating scale.

Table 13.3.   Numerical Rating Scale, Instrumental Music

Student's name _____ Date _____

Assignment _____

4 = student *always* performs task   3 = student *usually* performs task
2 = student *sometimes* performs task   1 = student *never* performs task

    A. Keeps sheet music in order
      4   3   2   1

    B. Proper posture
      4   3   2   1

    C. Keeps proper time to score
      4   3   2   1

    Student's score _____

Comments:

_____

Both the graphic and numerical rating scales can easily be adapted for self- or peer reviews. Table 13.6 is an example of the heading portion of a rating scale that can be used by the teacher, a peer, or the student. The individual simply checks the appropriate box, signs, and dates the instrument.

Table 13.4.   Descriptive Rating Scale, Instrumental Music

Student's name _____ Date _____

Assignment _____

Circle the word that shows how often the pupil did each of the behaviors listed.

    A. Keeps sheet music in order
      Never   Seldom   Usually   Always

    B. Proper posture
      Never   Seldom   Usually   Always

    C. Keeps proper time to score
      Never   Seldom   Usually   Always

Comments:

_____

Table 13.5.   Graphic Rating Scale, Instrumental Music

Student's name _____ Date _____

Assignment _____

Circle the symbol that shows how often the pupil did each of the behaviors listed.

◯   ⊕   ◇   △

Never   Seldom   Usually   Always

A. Keeps sheet music in order

◯   ⊕   ◇   △

B. Proper posture

◯   ⊕   ◇   △

C. Keeps proper time to score

◯   ⊕   ◇   △

Comments:

_____

⟨⟩ **Technology Excursion Trip**   *This rating scale was created by selecting Word and following the steps previously mentioned. The graphics on the rating scale were used by going to Insert, Picture, Autoshapes. You have a variety of choices from which to select. You can manipulate the "box" around the shape to make it as large or as small as you wish. You can also color the shape inside or color the outside line.*

RUBRICS

Rubrics are used to designate a score or numerical value to an assignment. There are three types of rubrics: analytical, holistic, and scoring. This chapter will only focus on the scoring rubric, which is defined as "brief, written descriptions of different levels of pupil performance. Rubrics can be used to summarize both pupil performances and products" (Airasian 1997: 231).

Rubrics can be considered as a descriptive rating scale. They consist of a series of "indicators" (closely tied to the measurable teaching objectives) that describe the criteria for the assignment or task. The indicators are given number values. When the teacher tabulates the student's grade, he or she adds up all the numbers for the grade.

Table 13.6.   Graphic Rating Scale for Teacher–Student–Peer Review, Instrumental Music

Student's name _____ Date _____

Assignment _____

Teacher Date _____ Signature _____

Student Date _____ Signature _____

Peer Date _____ Signature _____

Circle the symbol that shows how often the pupil did each of the behaviors listed.

$$\bigcirc \qquad \oplus \qquad \diamondsuit \qquad \triangle$$

Never   Seldom   Usually   Always

A. Keeps sheet music in order

$$\bigcirc \qquad \oplus \qquad \diamondsuit \qquad \triangle$$

B. Proper posture

$$\bigcirc \qquad \oplus \qquad \diamondsuit \qquad \triangle$$

C. Keeps proper time to score

$$\bigcirc \qquad \oplus \qquad \diamondsuit \qquad \triangle$$

Comments:

_____

Rubrics can be used for any performance-based task. They can be designed for a daily assignment, a project, or a test. Rubrics are a good evaluative tool for assigning a numerical grade to a student project. You can design the rubric to be scored by the teacher, student, or a peer by designating which individual is scoring at the top. Rubrics also provide a portion for comments by the scorer. "Rubrics are especially useful for setting pupil achievement targets and for obtaining a summative single score representation of pupil performance" (Airasian 1997: 232).

As an elementary classroom teacher and also as a university professor, I *always* gave the students the rubric *before* they completed the assignment. The students are the most important people in the classroom. There is no reason why they should be kept in the dark about what the grading criteria will be. I received positive feedback from students of all levels. Giving the scoring rubric to the students in advance alleviates much anxiety. It also thwarts that age-old question too often asked by students, "What does the teacher want me to do?" By giving the elementary students the criteria and rubric in advance, parents appreciated my efforts as well. Creating the scoring rubric prior to giving the assignment also helps the teacher to sit down and focus on specifically what will be entailed in this task or project. By putting down the criteria on paper, you will do a better job of explaining the criteria to the students. This will promote credibility with your students—a great example of a win/win situation.

Table 13.7 is a scoring rubric for an assignment in which the student will create a concept map (see the discussion about concept maps from chapter 2). This assignment could take a week or more to complete. Rather than the teacher running off worksheets for each element of this concept for every student, a single sheet is used for each student. Individual grades could be taken on level 1, level 2, level 3, and level 4. A "weighted grade" could be given to the entire assignment as a project or test grade. The option is left to the teacher.

As with all performance-based evaluations, please leave a space for comments by the teacher or evaluator. Students need both positive and constructive feedback.

Specifications for the work include the following:

- Center of concept will have the title "Battles of the Revolutionary War."
- You will include five aspects of level 1—write the names of the battles.
- Level 2 will include the name of today's state in which the battle occurred.
- Level 3 will include the name of the victor of that battle—the British or the colonists.
- Level 4 will include the name of the victorious general at that battle.

The student can see at a glance the point values for every criterion required for the project. By distributing this information to the student in advance, there is a full understanding on the part of the student as to the specific requirements for this project.

Table 13.8 presents a rubric that can be scored by the teacher, the student (self-assessment), or a peer. The individual completing the assessment can simply check the appropriate box and then add the date and signature.

Table 13.7. Rubric for Concept Map

BATTLES OF THE REVOLUTIONARY WAR
CONCEPT MAP

Student **Jane Doe**   U.S. History **6th Hour**   Date **October 20, 2**

CENTER
Shape contains title "Battles of the Revolutionary War"
(5 points)
CONCEPT MAP DESIGN—show four levels branching from center.
(20 points—5 points each)

LEVEL 1
Five shapes containing the names of five battles during the Revolutionary War
(25 points—5 points each)

LEVEL 2
Location—write the names of the present-day states in which the battles occurred.
(25 points—5 points each)

LEVEL 3
Who won? Write the names of the victor of the battle—the British or colonists.
(25 points—5 points each)

LEVEL 4
Write the name of the victorious general(s) at the battle (in some cases there may be more than one).
(25 points—5 points each)

Total Value—125 points

125–113 = A   112–100 = B   99–88 = C   87–76 = D   75–below = F

Comments:

CONCLUSION

Checklists, rating scales, and rubrics are used as performance-based evaluations. These tools can be utilized by the teacher, a peer, or as a self-evaluation. Checklists, rating scales, and rubrics are not to be used interchangeably. Each performance-based assessment has specific uses. Technology information included in this chapter will assist you in creating any of these performance-based assessments at home or at school using simple techniques found in Microsoft Word.

Table 13.8.   Concept Map Rubric for Teacher–Student–Peer Review

BATTLES OF THE REVOLUTIONARY WAR
CONCEPT MAP

Student **Jane Doe**   U.S. History **6th Hour**   Date received **October 20, 8**

Teacher Date _____ Signature _____

Student Date _____ Signature _____

Peer Date _____ Signature _____

CENTER
Shape contains title "Battles of the Revolutionary War"
(5 points)
CONCEPT MAP DESIGN—show four levels branching from center.
(20 points—5 points each)

LEVEL 1
Five shapes containing the names of five battles during the Revolutionary War
(25 points—5 points each)

LEVEL 2
Location—write the names of the present-day states in which the battles occurred.
(25 points—5 points each)

LEVEL 3
Who won? Write the names of the victor of the battle—the British or colonists.
(25 points—5 points each)

LEVEL 4
Write the name of the victorious general(s) at the battle (in some cases there may be more than one).
(25 points—5 points each)

Total Value—125 points

125–113 = A   112–100 = B   99–88 = C   87–76 = D   75–below = F

Comments:

REFERENCES

Airasian, P. W. 1997. *Classroom assessment.* 3d ed. New York: McGraw-Hill.

Linn, R. L., and N. E. Gronlund. 2000. *Measurement and assessment in teaching.* 8th ed. Upper Saddle River, N.J.: Merrill/Prentice Hall.

WEB REFERENCES

www.richland2.org/academics/GEMS/WriteTaskRubrics.html. Site for rubrics and tools for assessment.

www.grand.k12.ut.us/curric/rubrics.html. Also provides assessment tools and rubrics.

www.mich.com/~osborne/Steps_for_Creating_Rubrics.html. Describes "Basic Steps for Creating a Rubric."

www.projects.edtech.sandi.net/lewis/cajuns/Why%20rubrics.text.htm. Gives a rationale for using rubrics and also information for building a rubric.

http://mbhs.bergtraum.k12.ny.us/cybereng/rubric/. Offers rubrics.

www.sasked.gov.sk.ca/docs/ela/ela_list.html. Checklists and rating scales.

Student Portfolios

This chapter gives a basic overview of portfolios. If you are presently employed in a district that requires a portfolio system, the beginning section of this chapter will be beneficial to you. If you are a teacher education candidate, a practicing teacher in a district that does not require portfolios, or an alternative certification teacher, go on to the latter section of the chapter. This information will be practical and useful to you, your students, and their parents.

INTRODUCTION TO PORTFOLIOS

Many districts across the nation are using some form of student portfolios. These range from a simple file folder containing the student's work to an intricately designed purposeful authentic assessment.

> Ideally, portfolios are not just a static collection of what pupils have done. Rather, they provide opportunities for learners to organize a sample of their work, write reflective comments in their portfolios as they consider what they have done, and engage in written exchanges with their teacher about their progress and about content issues that interest and concern them. (Savage and Armstrong 2000: 389)

According to Linn and Gronlund (2000: 290), "Portfolios are sometimes described as portraits of a person's accomplishments. Using this metaphor, a student portfolio is usually a self-portrait, but one that often has benefited from guidance and feedback from a teacher and sometimes from other students." The "feedback from . . . other students" that Linn and Gronlund refer to are the peer evaluations placed in the portfolios.

The purpose of student portfolios is to show the students' progress, growth, and achievements *over time*—time being the duration of the school year. Linn and Gronlund (2000) believe that the two primary purposes for using portfolios are instruction and assessment. According to Wolfinger (2000: 285), "a portfolio is a collection of a student's achievements over a period of time as shown by a variety of different examples of student work. The main purpose of the portfolio is to show an individual student's growth over a period of time." Student portfolios can be a continuum of learning.

Perhaps you were required to create a teacher education portfolio before graduating from that prestigious university. If so, your portfolio could have included samples of your projects, letters of recognition, or photos of you student teaching. Wolfinger (2000) would describe these samples as "different examples" of your work as a teacher education candidate. The portfolio is particularly useful for students from diverse cultural backgrounds, students with learning problems, and gifted students, according to Tippins and Dana (1992). Students from diverse cultural backgrounds often have limited English language skills. A portfolio provides physical documentation of their growth throughout the school year. This documentation would go above and beyond the traditional paper-and-pencil tests.

> For the student who is mentally retarded or learning disabled, the use of the portfolio can give a more realistic picture of the student's learning. For the learner who is mentally retarded, the portfolio can show learning based on the individual's starting point rather than on some criterion established for average learners. A student's progress toward the goals established for the individual can be easily demonstrated. (Wolfinger 2000: 286)

A portfolio used with students with mental retardation or learning disabilities would showcase the goals of each student's IEP. The portfolio allows the gifted student to show his or her talents and abilities that surpass the average learner.

Portfolios are being required today by states and districts in specific curricular areas. Vermont was the first state to introduce portfolios as a primary state assessment. Portfolios in mathematics and writing were collected statewide for students in grades 4 and 8 (Linn and Gronlund 2000). The Pittsburgh Public School District worked at the district level to use portfolios to evaluate student writing in grades 6 through 12. Portfolios are used today throughout the country to assess students in virtually all curricular areas and also from the primary grades through the high school years.

If your state, district, or site uses student portfolios, follow the guidelines carefully. The parents and students will all be familiar with this process. As the new kid on the block, you will need to learn the parameters and follow them to the letter.

If your district does not use student portfolios, avoid this system like a bad plague. You will spend an enormous amount of time educating the students and parents about your intentions for this program, and there will be no follow-through next year. Save your energy for more important things, such as educating your students to the best of your ability.

PORTFOLIO PEARLS OF WISDOM

Welcome to the world of portfolios! In this section you will learn an option to the standard and highly structured student portfolio, this portrait of the student's accomplishments. You will learn how to implement a modified form that will benefit your students, impress your parents, and assist you during conferences. I write from professional experience in this section.

Rather than following the highly structured traditional portfolio style, you might wish to utilize a "modified portfolio" a few weeks before parent–teacher conferences. This system has been a lifesaver to me on numerous occasions during conferences. Look at your school calendar at the beginning of the school year, which will list important dates for the school year. Mark the dates for conferences and commit those dates to memory. As the rush of the school year begins, you will be thankful you marked the dates in advance. A few weeks before the conference date, begin a system to add a few papers to a simple file folder named the "Student Portfolio." Even primary-level students can participate in a modified or simplified portfolio system for a short time.

Show the students a simple manila file folder and explain to them that they will choose four papers (or whatever number you select in advance) that will be placed in this portfolio, which will be given to their parents during parent–teacher conferences. You will also choose the same number of papers to go inside the portfolio. Over the course of a few weeks, the portfolio will be filled with samples of the student's work to show and discuss during the conference. This simplified portfolio format will serve as a modified portrait of the student's accomplishments over a short time span.

I suggest to my teacher education candidates every semester the same proposal: Include items that can be included in a portfolio that are not "paper and pencil." Move away from the obvious toward the creative. Think outside that box! That list may include some of the following:

- An *audiocassette tape* of the student reading a story or giving a speech. Plan ahead—include an audiocassette tape with your student supply list at the beginning of the school year. Suggestion: Keep a running list in your plan book of items you wish to include *next* year for the student supply list. At the end of the school year, include these when you turn in your request for the beginning of the next school year. Your administrators and parents will be impressed with your organization at the beginning of the year, rather than asking for items throughout the year.

- A *computer disk* or *rewriteable CD* (CD-RW) containing digital camera photos of the student's completed project or artwork. One CD can hold the contents of 250,000 pages of text or a student's entire public or private school experience. Again, plan ahead—include one or more computer disks or one CD-RW with your student supply list at the beginning of the school year. You may be the only faculty member at your site who requests a CD-RW—very impressive.

- A *videotape* of the student completing a science experiment or working with a cooperative group project. Again, include a videotape when requesting your student supply list at the beginning of the school year.

Imagine how surprised the parents will be to see or hear one of these items rather than get to view a spelling test or a sample of handwriting!

The beauty of these suggestions is that they can be utilized fully with both the core curriculum and "elective" curricular areas. The three avenues of instructional documentation can also be used with a kindergarten student or with a high school student in advanced placement classes. An audiotape or videotape would be a wonderful resource to save information from music performances, speeches, or debates or to document learning a foreign language. Video clips could be saved to a CD-RW also. A computer disk or CD-RW would be best utilized with a family living course or the traditional shop course, not to mention art courses using any medium. Student work could be scanned and saved to a disk or CD-RW.

Drawbacks to the aforementioned suggestions are (1) equipment, (2) knowledge to use the equipment, and (3) time to use the equipment. The bare minimum equipment would be a computer, an audiocassette player, and a video camera. To save information to a CD-RW, the school would need to have a CD burner as a part of the computer. To create a top-of-the-line electronic portfolio, the hardware needed would include a computer with a CD burner, a video camera, a digital camera, and a color scanner. The elements of knowledge and time are up to the teacher. Optimally, the teacher can learn the pertinent technology skills through professional development training provided by the district. Wolfinger (2000) gives these further suggestions for inclusion in the student portfolio:

- *Peer reviews.* These are an assessment or evaluation of a student's work done by another student in the class. Generally the teacher creates a rubric, checklist, or rating scale that is completed by the student, another student, and the teacher. Samples of peer reviews are found in chapter 13.
- *Group reports or projects.* If the product of the group's work is a written document, copies of that document can be placed in the portfolio for each member of the group.
- *Photographs.* The best uses of photographic evidence are photographs that show how the project or activity developed from planning to final stages.
- *Computer printouts.* When students have the opportunity to use computer technology in the classroom, examples of their work should be included in the portfolio.
- *Student reflections.* The student's own evaluation of the samples of work in his or her portfolio can be included. A primary student could provide a reflection or summary on an audiotape or write a single-sentence summation. Older students can provide a more detailed written reflection.

Although this modified example is not the true form or purpose of a student portfolio, it will be an asset to you during the conference. As a new teacher, you will have actual papers to show the parents during their visit. Rather than *telling* them things about their child, you will be able to *show* them examples of their child's achievements. Whoever said that a picture (or paper) was worth a thousand words probably went through some difficult parent conferences before deciding on that motto. As an inexperienced teacher, this will give you credibility in the eyes of the parents. Quoting Martha Stewart here, "It's [credibility] a good thing."

What lies in the future for portfolios? Wolfinger (2000) believes that it is truly a cumulative record of student progress and should be added to each year the child is in school. Due to the volume of papers, he also suggests a technological alternative to the portfolio in the form of a laser disk portfolio in which the contents of the paper portfolio are transferred to a single laser disk. The disk would provide both an audio and visual record of the student's progress. A second option for future portfolios might be a rewriteable CD (CD-RW), which would have the capacity to store both audio and visual records of the student's progress. More teachers would have the opportunity to use a computer as opposed to a laser disk player to view student records.

CONCLUSION

You may obtain further information regarding portfolios by contacting the following location:

Portfolio News
Portfolio Assessment Clearinghouse
San Dieguito Union High School District
710 Encinitas Boulevard
Encinitas, California 92024
www.ed.gov/pubs/OR/ConsumerGuides/classuse.html

Winfield Cooper is editor of the quarterly *Portfolio News*, a publication of the Portfolio Assessment Clearinghouse. This publication provides twenty to thirty pages of articles, project briefs, and other materials by teachers, project directors, and researchers about local and state portfolio projects. It also serves as an information exchange for people interested in portfolios.

As indicated earlier, in Vermont fourth- and eighth-grade students are being assessed in writing and mathematics using three methods: a portfolio, a best piece from the portfolio, and a set of equivalent performance tasks. For more information regarding the Portfolio Project in Vermont, contact:

Commissioner of Education
Vermont Department of Education
Montpelier, Vermont 05602
(802) 828-3135
www.ed.gov/pubs/OR/ConsumerGuides/classuse.html

REFERENCES

Arter, J., V. Spandel, and R. Culham. 1995. Portfolios for assessment and instruction. *ERIC Digest.* Available at http://ericae.net/db/edo/ED388890.htm.

Baker, E. L., and R. L. Linn. 1992. *Writing portfolios: Potential for large-scale assessment.* Final report. Los Angeles: University of California, Center for Research on Evaluation, Standards, and Student Testing.

California Department of Education. 1994. *Golden State Examination science portfolio: A guide to teachers.* Sacramento: California Department of Education. Available at www.nwrel.org/eval/toolkit/folio.html.

Darling-Hammond, L., J. Ancess, and B. Falk. 1995. *Authentic assessment in action: Studies of schools and students at work.* New York: Teachers College Press.

Gerhart, M., J. L. Herman, E. L. Baker, and A. K. Whittaker. 1992. *Writing portfolios at the elementary level: A study of methods for writing assessment.* CSE Technical Report 337. Los Angeles: University of California, Center for Research on Education, Standards, and Student Testing. Available at www.cse.ucla.edu/.

Koretz, D., B. Stecher, S. Klein, and D. McCaffrey. 1994. *The evolution of a portfolio program: The impact and quality of the Vermont program in the second year.* CSE Technical Report 385. Los Angeles: University of California, Center for Research on Evaluation. Standards, and Student Testing. Available at www.cse.ucla.edu/.

Linn, R.L., and N. E. Gronlund. 2000. *Measurement and assessment in teaching.* 8th ed. Upper Saddle River, N.J.: Prentice Hall/Merrill.

Paulson, L. 1994. *Portfolio guidelines in primary math.* Portland, Ore.: Multnomah County Educational Service District. Available at www.nwrel.org/eval/toolkit/primary/html.

Savage, T. V., and D. G. Armstrong. 2000. *Effective teaching in elementary social studies.* 4th ed. Upper Saddle River, N.J.: Prentice Hall/Merrill.

Stecher, B., and K. J. Mitchell. 1995. *Portfolio-driven reform: Vermont teachers' understanding of mathematical problem solving and related changes in classroom practice.* CSE Technical Report 400. Los Angeles: University of California, Center for Research on Evaluation, Standards, and Student Testing. Available at www.cse.ucla.edu/.

Tippins, D. J., and N. F. Dana. 1992, March. Culturally relevant alternative assessment. *Science Scope* 51.

Wolfinger, D. M. 2000. *Science in the elementary and middle school.* New York: Addison Wesley Longman.

WEB REFERENCE

www.nwrel.org/scpd/sirs/6/cu11.html. Includes a number of links to additional websites that feature information about authentic assessment, with references to topics that include electronic portfolios, evaluating problem-solving processes, self-assessment in portfolios, and creating rubrics.

15

Standardized Testing and Curriculum Standards

This chapter is intended for the teacher education candidate as well as for those already working in classrooms. The topic of standardized testing goes hand-in-glove with curriculum standards—what content is covered on the standardized tests or the national curriculum standards for each curricular area.

Teachers in the field can follow the steps outlined for preparing your students and your classroom for testing sessions—before, during, and after standardized tests. Future teachers and teachers today can check the resources to obtain more information regarding the curricular standards.

American education has become more and more focused on the results from standardized tests over the past decades. The creativity of teachers and students is put on the back burner as state and national curriculum standards have come to the forefront. Newspapers publish standardized tests results. Community leaders use the testing information when promoting the school system to future citizens. These individuals focus on "what" is learned according to scores on standardized achievement tests. You will recall from reading chapter 3, several educational theorists and many educators choose to focus on "how" students learn.

As a teacher education adviser, I am often the first individual at the university who meets new or potential students. After I conduct transcript evaluations, the ladies and gentlemen begin to tell me the reason they want to be a teacher. I see faces light up, eyes sparkle, bright and shining smiles emerge. For these people, teaching is their lifelong dream. It is my job to help that dream become reality.

In all the formal and informal visits I have had with teacher education candidates, the responses are all centered on their love of children, their love of learning, and their desire to help make education—or the world—a better place. No one has ever shared their sincere desire to raise test scores at their school site. No teacher education candidate has ever longed and dreamed of thoroughly and sequentially covering all the curriculum standards prior to testing time. I have yet to meet a future teacher who wants to make the world a better place by topping the district in standardized test scores.

Think back to your favorite teachers when you were a student. If you met them today, what would you say to them? Would you tell them that they had a great impact in your life with those dittos or worksheets? Would you tell them that rote memorization of facts made you the individual you are today? Or would you discuss the project you completed, the play your group wrote and starred in, or how you enjoyed learning about life in faraway places? What type of teacher do you aspire to become? Teachers can use the teaching strategies and theories from Part I to teach concepts that students can transpose into correct answers on standardized tests. "Formal testing and grading systems have many important functions in education; however, developing the genius of students doesn't happen to be one of them" (Armstrong 1998: 35). The genius of students is achieved through creative teaching strategies and practices—minus the worksheets and drills. These same strategies can be assessed through a myriad of testing practices.

When the teacher education candidates or alternative certification candidates become classroom teachers, visions of grandeur are replaced by a strong dose of today's reality. They learn the enormous and paramount importance placed on standardized test results—by the board of education, by the superintendent, by the building-level principal, and at times by the parents. Every classroom teacher needs a sign on his or her desk that reads "The Buck Stops Here," just as Harry Truman had during his presidency. This emphasis on test results is similar to the statue of Atlas working hard to balance the world on his shoulders. Classroom teachers are balancing all the curriculum standards—national, state, and district standards—along with every other responsibility of managing a class of students on their shoulders.

"Teaching to the test" is not condoned. Concepts can be taught using a variety of instructional strategies (see chapter 2, "Teaching Strategies to Help Students Learn"), which appeal to the learning modalities (see chapter 1 on

"Learning Modalities—How Do Children Learn?") and enhance learning. The concept of learning is different from the basic recall of an answer on a test. The following information will help the classroom teacher prepare the students, parents, and the classroom for standardized tests—before, during, and after the testing session.

NORM-REFERENCED AND CRITERION-REFERENCED TESTS

Standardized tests can be broadly categorized into two groups: norm-referenced tests and criterion-referenced tests. A *norm-referenced test* (NRT) is "designed to measure individual differences in achievement, intelligence, interests, attitudes, or personality" (Sax 1997: 16). Kellough (1996) refers to norm-referenced grading as "educationally dysfunctional." Remember from your college days the old practice of grading on a curve? That practice is norm-referenced grading. Students are compared and ranked. Norm-referenced tests are useful when comparing student performance to that of others at the same age or same grade level (statewide or nationally).

If your class takes a norm-referenced test, most likely they will be "normed" statewide and also nationally. It is very easy to set a goal of improving test scores by a certain number of percentile points. Making any improvement on a nationally normed test is extremely difficult. You will not have the same students from one year to the next. One hundred percent of your students will not be at peak form on the day of that particular test.

Criterion-referenced tests (CRTs) "relate a student's score on an achievement test to a domain of knowledge rather than to another student's score" (Sax 1997: 17). They compare student performance with an absolute standard called a *criterion*.

Technically the same test can be scored as a norm-referenced test and also as a criterion-referenced test. One of the questions I always pose to my test and measurements students is the following:

Every sixth grade student in Okarche, Oklahoma, took a test on January 30, 2005. There are 250 sixth graders in Okarche. One-half of the tests were sent to OSU for graduate students to score the test as a criterion-referenced test. One-half of the tests were sent to OU for graduate students to score the test as a norm-referenced test. How is it possible for the same examination to be scored in two different manners?

It is possible to give students the *same* test—same questions, same format, same test—and score it differently. Go back and read the descriptions of norm-referenced and criterion-referenced tests once again. You will see how this is possible—perhaps not economically feasible for public schools, but possible nonetheless.

Individuals often make the mistake of comparing test scores from one year to the next. Be sure you are comparing the same manufactured test, such as the Iowa Test of Basic Skills. You cannot compare one year of criterion-referenced test scores and the next year of norm-referenced test scores—they are as different as bananas and apples. Both are tests, but they are not identical tests. They cannot be compared from one year to the next.

STANDARDIZED TESTING—BEFORE, DURING, AND AFTER

Classroom teachers must prepare their students to take standardized tests. The information in table 15.1 will help you to prepare your students—and yourself—for standardized tests in three phases—before, during, and after. Let's look at these tips in great detail.

Assist your students to become "student friendly" with multiple-choice questions and "bubble" answer sheets. You have the responsibility to prepare your students to take standardized tests. You know that the vast majority of the questions will be in a multiple-choice form. You can begin the first week of school creating multiple-choice questions for your students and asking them to use a "bubble sheet" to record their answers. This can be done with virtually any subject area. Your students will become familiar with this form of question and also become familiar with using a bubble sheet.

Rather than creating major assessments using bubble answers, you might consider one question per day. The students can self-check their answers at the end of the week, thus using only one answer sheet per week.

Table 15.1.   Before, During, and After Testing

1. Assist your students to become "student-friendly" with multiple-choice questions and bubble answer sheets.
2. Know the standards you are responsible for teaching *and* know your time span for completion at the beginning of the year.
3. Teach the standards as concepts using real-life experiences as examples.
4. Notify parents in advance of testing dates.
5. Prepare your classroom so that it is "standardized test ready."
6. Testing sessions—you will survive.
7. Reward your students after test time.

A suggestion for teachers working with students who are unfamiliar with bubble sheets is to start with larger-sized bubbles. I taught third grade the first year that those students were required to take the Oklahoma Criterion Reference Test. Every week we took a spelling pretest on Wednesday. I created a test sheet in a multiple-choice format. I also gave them bubble sheets that had rather large bubbles for them to mark their answers. As the year progressed, I used the "reduction" portion of the photocopying machine to make the bubbles smaller. When they took the standardized tests in the spring, they were not the least bit intimidated about using bubble sheets (standardized answer sheets) or seeing spelling questions in a multiple-choice format. This sequential step approach would work well with students with learning problems or visual perception problems.

The second tip is to know the standards you are responsible for teaching, *and* know your time span for completion at the beginning of the year. Another way to prepare your students for standardized tests is to pay close attention to the curriculum standards—the national, state, or district standards. "The National Council on Education Standards and Testing has recommended that national standards for subject matter content in education be developed for all core subjects—the arts, civics/social studies, English/language arts/reading, geography, history, mathematics, and science" (Kellough 1996: 72).

Curriculum standards are guidelines, generally written in an objective form, that are grouped by curricular discipline and then by grade level. Kellough (1996) defines *standards* as "a definition of what students should know and be able to do." They are concepts that students in each grade level should know. The question arises as to *when* the students should know these curriculum standards. If the standardized test is given *during* the school year over these curriculum standards, then the students should be prepared by test time.

Most districts will supply faculty members with a set of required standards at the beginning of the year. Keep in mind that these standards or curriculum guidelines have been designed to correspond with the standardized tests your students will be taking during the year.

If you do not receive a set of standards at the beginning of the year, take the initiative and ask your principal to supply you with one. If one is not readily available, you can write to your state Department of Education for a copy. For immediate results, you can use chapter 24, "Fill in Your Gaps—Professional Development," as a reference. Find the website for the organization of the curricular discipline you teach, and learn the national standards for that discipline. The national, state, and district standards will be similar.

A very good general website on the national standards and also the state standards is at the following address: www.education-world.com/standards/national/index.shtml. This site offers easy access to the national curricular organizations, the national standards, and the state standards.

After you have obtained the set of national, state, and/or district standards, how do you plan to keep them organized? I supervised a first-year teacher who taught several grade levels of special education students. She also taught in a large district that had created a set of district standards. This teacher was juggling two sets of standards for each curricular level for three different grades. In her grade book she had a tab for third-grade reading. I opened the book to find grades for the third graders in reading, then the state standards for reading for third graders, then the district's standards for reading for third graders. Her book was organized in this fashion for each curricular area she taught. Then she moved to fourth-grade reading, and the format continued. Then fifth-grade reading.... Tabs divided each section for easy access.

Rather than trying to keep track of a grade book, a state standards book, and a district standards book, this teacher had taken the books apart and put them together in a three-ring binder. Her organization at the beginning of the school year had made her entire year run much more smoothly.

For those of you teaching different subjects or different grade levels, consider color-coding your organizational system. This will allow you easy access to your information. Also the use of tabs will be helpful. Consider making your own tabs from Post-It notes trimmed to the size you need. They can be easily adjusted to maintain visibility, and they also come in a array of colors to make color-coding easy.

Once you have organized your standards, consider creating a time line for completion of these standards. Many first-year teachers I supervise have the misconception that this information is to be covered by the end of the school year. I quickly correct this misconception. Ask your principal *when* the standardized tests will be given to your students. Some states have a "window" or span of three or four weeks within which the tests must be given. The district will then select one week inside that window. Your principal has been attending the administrative meetings in which that information is shared.

When you have a month and weeks as your guide, make careful examination of the standards that are required of your students. Create your own time line for teaching and assessing those concepts. Leave time to review the concepts prior to the testing week. (Your time line will be different if the testing month is different from March.) Table 15.2 is a calendar time line for a school that begins in August and tests in March. Note that the beginning of January will be used for reteaching and reviewing concepts taught just after the winter break.

The concepts are to be *learned* by testing time. The standards are to be transformed to appeal to both the left and right brain–dominant students. Through instructional strategies, this material is to be taught to appeal to all three learning modalities. These objectives are to be dissected and assembled once again to promote learning—learning not by the end of the year but by the time that the standardized tests are given. I tell my first-year teachers to learn the standards and commit them to memory. Put the content into the form of projects, group activities, research projects, and all other instructional ways that will promote and retain learning.

The third tip is to teach the standards as concepts using real-life experiences as examples. Build a bridge between what is relevant and real to the student and the concept. Use those manipulatives, graphics, and visuals. Appeal to the kinesthetic, visual, and auditory learners.

Consider the concept of "computing the area of a rectangle." Students can be taught the formula for this task and then use it with a set of numbers. A savvy classroom teacher will go beyond the mathematical formula and give real-life examples to which the students can relate.

I used the Fisher-Price farm, dollhouse, and schoolhouse with my elementary mathematics methods class. The students were placed into groups and asked to use the formula for finding the area of a rectangle to find the area (square footage) of these toys. We measured in centimeters rather than inches. They were ready to take the concept further to measure the walls and the roof.

Table 15.2.   Time Line for Teaching Objectives Prior to Standardized Testing

Aug.	Sept.	Oct.	Nov.	Dec.	Jan. *reteach first week after winter break	Feb.	March *review concepts prior to test date

We took a simple concept and put it into a real-life situation. The visual and kinesthetic learners in the classroom enjoyed the activity. The auditory learning modality was addressed when the students reported on their measurements and how they computed the area.

Fourth, notify parents in advance of testing dates. The district will take on this responsibility. Your building principal will include this information in the newsletter and post it on the school marquee. Still there will be parents who did not receive this notification. As a professional, you should also include this information with your class calendar or newsletter. Use your word-processing skills to create a special information flyer to send home to parents. Figure 15.1 is a sample of a communication to be sent home to parents informing them about the standardized testing sessions that will be coming within several months. Parents will have the opportunity to mark these dates on their home calendars for future reference. Figure 15.2 is a sample of a communication to be sent home a week before the testing week begins.

FIGURE 15.1
General information letter to parents

> Dear Parents,
>
> I realize that our standardized testing sessions are scheduled several months away, but I wanted to let you know the dates. Please reserve Monday, March 1, through Thursday, March 4, on your calendars at home. Any makeup examinations will be given on Friday, March 5. We would appreciate scheduling any appointments for your child on a week prior to or after our testing week.
>   Thank you in advance for your cooperation.
>
> **Mr. Jones**

FIGURE 15.2
Specific information letter to parents

> Dear Parents,
>
> Your child will be taking standardized examinations during the week of March 1 through March 5. Please be sure that your child has two or three #2 pencils with good erasers. Thank you.
>
> **Mr. Jones**

The next tip is to prepare your classroom so that it is "standardized test ready." Look closely at your room and make a checklist of things to do to get your room ready for testing.

- *Windows.* If your classroom has windows, close the blinds or curtains.
- *Doors.* If your door has a glass panel, cover the panel with paper. This will prevent any distractions in the classroom.
- *Seating arrangement.* Examine your current seating arrangement closely. How can you rearrange the desks and chairs to best facilitate a testing environment? If the desks are grouped together, put them in the traditional rows for the testing time frame. Ask colleagues how they arrange their students' seating to accommodate test sessions.
- *Visual distractions within the classroom.* Remove any posters or bulletin boards that might include answers to the test questions. Make your classroom a distraction-free testing environment.
- *Auditory distractions within the classroom.* Many schools today have centralized heating and air conditioning. The classroom teacher cannot adjust the temperature. If your classroom has a unit that allows you to adjust the controls, consider setting the control to "Fan" rather than "Auto." This will allow the fan to run continuously through the testing session, creating a dull sound that will alleviate much noise in the room. Readjust the setting back to "Auto" after the testing session.

  Another strategy is to use a box fan. Place the fan one to two feet away from the back wall in your classroom. Face the fan *toward* the wall. Turn the fan to the lowest setting. This will also create a dull sound that will assist in "sound control" in your room. You can try this out in the classroom before test time. You might want to adjust to another setting to achieve the sound quality you wish.
- *Outside your classroom.* Post a large sign on your door that reads "TESTING." You might want to add "Please do not enter." The entire school will be aware that this is testing week, but a sign on the door will help prevent any interruptions. Remove the sign when your students have completed their testing session for the day.

Be sure that all is ready prior to the testing sessions. Create a checklist if necessary to be sure you are prepared. Have extra #2 pencils sharpened and ready. Read through your testing booklet in advance. Often the teacher will need to supply the students with plain photocopying paper for the test. If this is needed, have it in your classroom on test day ready to give to your students.

Know in advance whether you have a student who takes medication or any sessions, such as physical therapy or a breathing treatment, at the time that you have scheduled your standardized tests. Check with the school nurse, counselor, or school secretary for this information. Adjust your test time to best accommodate all students in the classroom.

Finally, reward your students after test time. Consider the options you have for rewarding your students as well as the financial cost involved to you. When you have determined a few choices, give the students their options and vote as a class. This will give them a sense of ownership in selecting their reward.

My students often took standardized tests during the week of March 17—St. Patrick's Day. I created a "snack schedule" in which the students would bring a specific snack on a specific day. On St. Patrick's Day, our theme was "Anything Green." Students brought pickles, celery, green doughnuts, green bagels, salads—any snack that included something green. The students really enjoyed this.

Another day on our snack schedule was "Crackers and _____." The students could bring any type of cracker and something to go with it such as cheese or peanut butter. Again we had very unique combinations of snacks.

CONCLUSION

Standardized testing and curriculum standards go hand in hand. Teacher education candidates and also teachers in the field need to have a hard copy of the standards in a well-organized format. Several steps were given in this chapter to help teachers prepare students and the classroom for standardized tests—before, during, and after the tests.

More and more emphasis has been placed on standardized test results in recent years. With the No Child Left Behind Act and other legislation coming in the future, even more accountability will be on educators. Although no individual ever enters the teaching profession with the goal of "topping the charts" on standardized testing, student achievement measured by standardized test results is a responsibility to be shared by all educators.

The evaluation of students comes in many forms. Just as lesson plans involves much decision making, so does the evaluation process. Always tie the evaluation questions back to the daily measurable teaching objectives.

To receive more information or a hard copy of the national standards by discipline, please contact the following:

- *Civics*: Center for Civic Education, 5146 Douglas Fir Road, Calabasas, California 91302
- *Social studies*: National Council for the Social Studies (NCSS), 3501 Newark Street, NW, Washington, D.C. 20016
- *English/reading/language arts*: Center for the Study of Reading, 174 Children's Research Center, 51 Gerty Drive, Champaign, Illinois 61820
- *Geography*: Geography Standards Project, 1600 M Street, NW, Washington, D.C. 20036
- *History*: National Center for History in the Schools at UCLA, 231 Moore Hall, 405 Hilgard Avenue, Los Angeles, California 90024

REFERENCES

Airasian, P. 1997. *Classroom assessment.* 3d ed. New York: McGraw-Hill.

Armstrong, T. 1998. *Awakening genius in the classroom.* Alexandria, Va.: Association for Supervision and Curriculum Development.

Sax, G. 1997. *Principles of educational and psychological measurement and evaluation.* 4th ed. Belmont, Calif.: Wadsworth.

Linn, R. L., and N. E. Gronlund. 2000. *Measurement and assessment in teaching.* 8th ed. Upper Saddle River, N.J.: Merrill/Prentice Hall.

WEB REFERENCES

www.ed.gov and www.nclb.gov. No Child Left Behind Act of 2001.
    www.nochildleftbehind.gov. Presents an introduction to the No Child Left Behind Act.

www.whitehouse.gov. Includes a "Fact Sheet: No Child Left Behind Act."

ASSESSMENT

One of the best-practice suggestions from Part III was information to obtain copies of curriculum standards. These standards will be your framework for planning objectives to enhance student learning. You can incorporate the information from Parts I and II with the standards.

When you are creating your rubrics, rating scales, checklists, and communications to parents for grade reports, always remember to utilize technology. This is the fastest and most efficient way to save and retrieve data. When you begin to create your professional portfolio (discussed in Part VI), your created information can become part of your portfolio. This information can also become part of a detailed resume for future employers. Take time now to save the data for future use.

DAILY CLASSROOM DUTIES

I am a teacher. A teacher is someone who leads. There is no magic here. I do not walk on water. I do not part the sea. I just love children.

—*Marva Collins*

The importance of designing a smoothly running classroom is paramount. Suggestions within this section will assist the teacher both at the beginning of the school year and throughout the year.

Classroom Rules

This chapter is designed for all three intended reading groups. Teacher education candidates will see evidence throughout the chapter of the vast importance of using forethought when planning for daily classroom duties. Teachers, including those who have come through a traditional teacher education program as well as alternative certification teachers, will read tips and suggestions for creating an effectively maintained classroom. Research is presented on effective and ineffective teaching practices that will promote a classroom conducive to learning, rather than one prone to disturbances.

When I studied for my undergraduate and graduate degrees in the 1970s, we covered every aspect of teaching except the topic of discipline. In my administrative studies, I learned how to avoid lawsuits involving corporal punishment and denial of due process. I learned how to check a student's IEP to determine the appropriate consequence (punishment) for special services students. My professors used the verb *document* or noun *documentation* three times when the topic of covering your tracks came into play. They emphasized careful and detailed record keeping.

In all my studies, I never learned how to create a classroom, sitewide, or districtwide discipline policy. In my years as a classroom teacher, however, I had the opportunity to be a part of one district that took the steps to develop a districtwide discipline policy. The district brought in a facilitator to teach *every* teacher about a specific discipline philosophy. We developed our classroom plan, which coincided with a site plan. If parents had more than one child at our site, the plan was basically the same. Children need consistency; parents love consistency. Our district was on its way to many successes.

First-year teachers may walk into a school that has had a sitewide plan in effect for several years. The students and parents know this plan well. Therefore, the teacher only needs to educate a tiny handful of students who are new to the school about the expectations regarding school and classroom rules. Rejoice and give thanks for those who came before you to iron out all the wrinkles of this plan.

ESTABLISHING CLASSROOM RULES

Before any type of discipline plan can be put into effect, you first must establish classroom rules. If you are part of a site that does not have a set of unified rules, you will be responsible for establishing your classroom rules. You can go to the nearest school supply store and purchase a set of colorful and elegantly printed rules (which the manufacturer designed), or you can roll up your sleeves and create your own.

Begin by asking your colleagues about their classroom plans, which is a simple and often-overlooked option. The teachers who work with students at your same grade level or same curricular discipline can be a wealth of help. When I served as the university representative for a middle school science teacher, she had every necessary facet of the class in order except laboratory rules. Often when teachers vary from the regular classroom setting, a different set of rules is necessary. She checked with her colleagues for the lab rules that had been established several years earlier.

Some teachers already have a mental set of rules filed away. They ask the students for input in establishing the rules while steering and guiding the conversation to a point where all the rules in their mental file cabinets come into play. The rules were discussed and set by the class. These are *class* rules. Sometimes the teacher will write the rules on a poster and have every student sign them. This promotes *ownership* of the rules. Absolutely every person involved in some aspect of education enjoys giving input. Why not allow the students some? I have a dear friend who has taught kindergarten for a zillion years. She's had the same classroom rules every year! The students keep making the same suggestions—with a little help from the teacher.

Some teachers prefer to create their own set of classroom rules. If this is your preference, here are some guidelines:

- *Use five or fewer rules.* These are elementary, middle school, or high school students. They can keep only track of a few rules. Rocket scientists, on the other hand, can keep track of more than five rules. Remember: five rules or less for students, more than five for rocket scientists!

- *Number your rules.* When a student breaks a rule, write down his or her name and the number of the rule on the chalkboard. Before the chalkboard is erased at the end of the day, write down the student's name and the rule number in the last vertical column in your lesson plan book. The samples shown in chapter 6 had a section for "agenda." Information such as the student's name and rule number could be placed in this section of the lesson plan book. This placement would automatically show the date as well. This is a form of documentation, documentation, documentation. Over time a pattern may emerge, such as Susan has come without homework five times in the past two weeks. You know not only the number of times Susan has come unprepared but also the dates just by looking at the code in your lesson plan book. A small bit of effort produces a credible teacher who can produce verification of a problem. Quite impressive for a professional! When you contact the parent, counselor, or administrator, you have valid dates and frequencies easily at hand.

- *Create* measurable *rules.* I would like for every student (and adult, for that matter) to be honest. Neither you nor I can determine with 100 percent accuracy whether the student is indeed telling the truth; therefore, do not use "Be honest" or "Always tell the truth" as one of your rules. You just cannot measure it. "Brings pencils, paper, books, and homework to class everyday" can be measured easily. Stick with the *objective* rather than *subjective* rules. Remember in college when you took a multiple-choice test opposed to an essay test? The multiple-choice approach was *objective* grading; the essay test was *subjective* grading. There is very little area for dispute or debate when using measurable objective rules, from either students or parents.

     Consider your unique situation. If you are the technology teacher, you have unique concerns about the care of the equipment. If you are the instrumental music teacher, you are genuinely concerned about the condition and security of the instruments as well as the organization of the sheet music. Include these specific needs as part of your classroom rules.

DISPLAYING YOUR CLASSROOM RULES

After you have established your classroom rules, you need to have them approved by the principal. Please make your building administrator aware of your rules and seek his or her approval before proceeding.

Most districts require teachers to "post" their rules in the classroom. I used one 8½ by 11-inch page for each rule and then copied them onto colored paper before putting them in sets around the room. You may choose to use a large piece of poster board for all the rules. Whichever form you choose, be certain the writing is large and bold so it can be seen from a distance. Printing all the rules on one sheet of paper in twelve-point font will not be acceptable.

Post or display the rules on all four walls in the classroom. Often teachers like to change the seating arrangement throughout the school year. Sometimes the "front" of the room changes. If students are arranged in a grouped seating arrangement, not everyone is facing the same direction. Therefore, post your rules on every wall in your room. A small amount of effort will cover all the bases. Professionals go the extra mile to accommodate every student.

CONSEQUENCES

Following the approval of your classroom rules, you need to establish a set of corresponding consequences. Take into consideration the age/maturity level of your students. You would not ask a first grader to write a two-page essay. Consider writing a sentence or paragraph (I kept the writing assignments in a marked envelope in my plan book), missing a portion of recess (which is difficult to track), or trying a more creative approach. For example, one of my wildest consequences was to ask the student to be the last person served in the cafeteria.

Just as you post your classroom rules, you also need to post your consequences in some fashion. Obviously this could be on the same piece of poster board. You will also seek approval of your consequences from the principal.

Please plan your consequences in advance. If you wish for the child to miss a designated number of minutes of recess, how can you determine whether this was accomplished? Some teachers on my faculty would send out a slip of paper for me to sign when I had recess duty. I never had a pencil or pen with me on the playground. It is also difficult for the teacher on duty who is watching a few hundred children to keep track of how many minutes your specified child is supposed to sit out. The concept of missing recess is much easier said than done. Think this through.

STUDENTS PARTICIPATE IN THE DOCUMENTATION PROCESS

Some theorists and university professors challenge the idea of students writing for disciplinary purposes—writing sentences as a consequence. Sometimes I am asked my position on this subject as a university professor for teacher education majors. I consistently sympathize with a classroom teacher attempting to show some initiative in dealing with disruptive students. I wonder how recently those theorists were in the trenches working day in and day out with students.

Why not request that the student participate in the documentation process? It involves some writing on the student's part. It allows the classroom teacher to continue—uninterrupted—the instructional process. The end result is a student-completed form to be kept in a file for documentation. Plan ahead for the designated location where the documentation will be kept. The student goes over and removes a form from an envelope or folder, completes it, and turns it in.

If one of your rules is "Come prepared with pencil, paper, books, and assignments each day," create a form that reflects that rule. You may want to just select a portion of that rule to document. Figure 16.1 is a general example to document "student nonproduction"—student does not have assignment.

You can detail or streamline this basic form to best meet your needs. A teacher with over one hundred students may wish to add a place for the student to circle the "hour" or "period" in which he or she is in class. Teachers who teach several different subjects during the day may wish to include these subjects on the form so that the student simply circles or checks the

FIGURE 16.1
Basic documentation template

Date assignment was given _____ Assignment due _____

Subject _____

Was class time given to complete this assignment? Yes/No

Location of assignment _____

Student's signature _____ Today's date _____

correct subject. Figure 16.2 shows a more streamlined documentation form.

There are several advantages to this system. Some responsibility is placed on the student. The teacher is able to proceed with instruction of the entire group of students. Learning continues for the group. The end result of documentation is achieved. The teacher has credible verification to show the principal or parent. Rather than attempting to remember how many times Johnny has committed an offence this week, the teacher once again has documentation, documentation, documentation. In this particular case, you have the student's own handwriting on the documentation.

HOW DO YOU GET THOSE DUCKS IN A ROW?

How do you put the rules, consequences, documentation, and any other daily tasks together into a tightly knit package? How do you get all those ducks in a row? Before you start searching websites for "duck-herding procedures," consider the following information. One of the goals of this book is to help you become a creative, innovative, effective, thinking-out-of-the-box teacher, but we still have to sweat the small stuff regarding daily classroom duties. An examination of traits, qualities, or characteristics of effective teachers is a good place to start.

FIGURE 16.2
Detailed documentation template

Complete the following form. Place your form in the pocket in the back of the folder.

Check the correct hour regarding this assignment.
_____ 1st Hour/Algebra I   _____ 2d Hour/Algebra II   _____ 3d Hour/Algebra I
_____ 4th Hour/Math   _____ 5th Hour/Algebra II   _____ 6th Hour/Math II

Assignment was page _____ Problem numbers _____

Date assignment was given _____ Assignment due _____

Was class time given to complete this assignment? Yes/No

Number of class sessions devoted to this assignment _____

Present location of assignment _____

Student's signature _____ Today's date _____

Much research has been done on the topic of teacher effectiveness. Borich (2000) concludes that effective teachers

> established themselves as instructional leaders early in the school year. They worked on rules and procedures until students learned them. Instructional content was important for these teachers, but they also stressed group cohesiveness and socialization, achieving a common set of classroom norms. By the end of the first three weeks, they were ready for the rest of the year. (378)

The following highlights put the findings of Emmer, Evertson, and Anderson (1980) into laymen's terms:

- Come prepared to teach. Don't just show up—arrive prepared and ready to teach. Students of any age can easily detect when the teacher is unprepared—even four-year-olds! You will have fewer classroom disturbances and interruptions if you are prepared.
- Work until all the students have *learned* the rules and procedures. Major and repeated efforts have been made to help the student learn this information. Remember the famous quote: "What is covered is not necessarily what is learned." Don't just go over a topic or cover it once; work on it until the students have learned it. You will have fewer classroom disturbances if the students know their boundaries and your expectations.
- Build community. Conduct several activities in which the students have the opportunity to get to know their fellow classmates. Remember the motto of the Three Musketeers: One for all and all for one! A second bonus is while the students are learning about each other, the teacher is also learning valuable information about each student. Building community has many other bonuses. You will have fewer classroom disturbances if the classroom environment is conducive to learning and community.
- After a short time, the group is ready to focus on a successful year. Time on task learning the rules, procedures, and teacher expectations is time well spent. This will promote fewer classroom disturbances.

The procedures from the study by Emmer et al. could include fire, tornado, or earthquake drills or even basic site rules such as procedures involving lunch responsibilities or rules for loading buses at the end of the day. How does the teacher keep track of who is out of the room? The traditional hall pass procedure would be another to include. These procedures are basic expectations by the teacher and school to get the student through the day.

Just as Emmer et al. examined the effective qualities of teachers that they termed "good managers," they also made conclusions about teachers who were considered "poor managers." The latter can also fall into my personally created category of "nonorganized," which means that there is no evidence whatsoever that any form of organization has been made by the teacher. Simply stated, the following conclusions can be made of less effective teachers who are poor managers:

- The daily routine is not carefully planned—it just happens. Rather than staying in a proactive mode, poorly organized teachers are reactive or reactionary. They do not have all their ducks in a row!
- The students are clueless regarding classroom rules and procedures. Perhaps there was a mention of some rules once on the first day of school, but that portion of class time has flown over the majority of the students' heads.
- Less effective teachers are poor monitors. Do not stand at the podium and lecture to students and expect the learners to remain "engaged." They will zone out before your eyes! If you need the assistance of your teacher's edition, pick it up from the podium and carry it as you circulate around the room. Your feet are not embedded in cement in front of that podium! Monitor during whole- or small-group time on task. Monitor during tests. Monitor during roll call. Be up and visible to the students.
- The consequences of poor behavior are inconsistent, and if offered, they are delivered in an untimely manner. This ties back to the first characteristic. Poor planning on the part of the teacher affects many aspects of the daily routine. The ducks are still not in a row!

CONCLUSION

This chapter has emphasized the important task of creating classroom rules and expectations. Careful planning and thoughtful teaching of these rules will be a cornerstone in creating a classroom conducive to learning.

REFERENCE

Borich, G. D. 2000. *Effective teaching methods*. 4th ed. Upper Saddle River, N.J.: Prentice Hall/Merrill.

Emmer, E. T., C. M. Evertson, and L. M. Anderson. 1980. Effective classroom management at the beginning of the school year. *Elementary School Journal* 80, no. 5: 219–31.

17

Class Incentives

This chapter is intended for all three readerships. Teachers in the field will glean ideas and procedures for class incentives. Teacher education candidates will gather possible ideas to use when they have their own classrooms.

Class incentives are methods used by teachers to motivate students, either for a period of time or throughout the duration of the school year. Incentives can involve every student in the school or just the students in your class.

School incentives can be grouped into two categories: intrinsic and extrinsic rewards. "Intrinsically motivated actions are performed out of interest and require no external prods," according to Edwards (2000: 308). Extrinsic motivation has a "carrot at the end of the stick"—some incentive, usually a tangible one. Translating the topic of intrinsic and extrinsic rewards to teachers, I would say that a teacher who works for the love of the profession is motivated intrinsically. A teacher who works hard to earn a bonus based on the standardized test results of his or her students is extrinsically motivated. That financial bonus is an extrinsic reward.

Student incentives abound on the Internet. Students are rewarded with insurance discounts, travel discounts, and discounts on various purchases such as office supplies.

Some school sites will have a short-term all-school incentive program. An example is a canned food drive in which the class that brings in the most cans wins some item or some privilege. Volunteers usually monitor these short-term drives. If, by chance, you find yourself on a planning committee for such a project, keep the responsibilities of the classroom teacher to a minimum.

Everyone on the planet likes to receive a reward of some type. We all are looking for that carrot at the end of the stick. Class incentives are a great way to encourage your students as a collective group. The ideas for class incentives are endless. Here are just a few:

- *Praise or compliment chain.* Put together a paper chain every time the class receives verbal praise or a compliment. Stretch the chain from the ceiling to the floor or from one side of the room to the other. When your chain attains the desired length, the entire class will receive some reward.
- *Buttons in a jar, marbles in a jar, cotton balls in a jar*—something *in a jar!* Each time the class does something marvelous (e.g., arriving quietly from recess), place an item in a jar. When the jar is filled, the entire class will receive a reward.
- *Tally marks for the week.* The class receives a tally mark each time they are magnificent. At the end of the week, they receive the number of minutes for extra recess to correspond with the number of tally marks. Check with your principal for approval on this one. Some principals do not want extra recesses. Also have a plan B in case of inclement weather.
- *Gumball machine poster.* Each time the class is wonderful, they receive a colored circle sticker placed on a gumball machine poster. When the poster is filled, it's party time!

GETTING STARTED

Many teachers will design several reward or incentive options and get approval from the principal before discussing things with the class. Consider cost and also the resources you have on hand or can easily access. As I have mentioned previously, students enjoy being involved in the decision-making process. Present a few options to your class, allow time for discussion, and ask them to vote on their favorite choice. By making the students part of the decision-making process, they will be greatly motivated to attain the class incentive. They will have a feeling of "ownership" in the process and in the outcome.

You will see various types of incentives in elementary classrooms today. Almost every researcher advises against removing a sticker, tally mark, or marble if the class is less than wonderful. Always give rather than take away! That's a good motto in the classroom and also in life.

Be creative with your classroom reward. We live in an age of videos in every household. The easiest reward (i.e., a "no-brainer") is to show a video. Use some gray matter between your ears and come up with something magnificent. Try something far-out such as a beach party, complete with beach blankets and Beach Boys music in the dead of winter (inside, of course). Keep interest and spirits high! Reward your students for excellence.

When selecting a day for your reward, consider whether your incentive is to be indoors or outdoors. It will be simple to select a time and day for an inside activity; outside is much more difficult. Design a plan B for an outside reward—either a backup date or a backup location. Notify the parents of this day amply ahead of time. They may need to make schedule changes in order for their child to attend. Also select a time in which every student may attend. Work around any pull-outs such as receiving physical therapy or meeting with the counselor.

Class incentives are easier than individual student incentives. It is difficult to keep track of each child throughout the day. Also individual incentives can be considered subjective. Get your feet wet with a class incentive first.

One consideration to view long and hard is to continue the incentive process when the teacher is absent. As a substitute teacher, I remember feeling confused and bewildered by a class of first graders who wanted me to put a handful of something into a jar. There was nothing in the lesson plans about this "jar thing," nothing in the substitute folder. I chose to postpone the incentive program until the teacher returned. Plan ahead. Do not put a stranger in charge of your classroom incentives.

CONCLUSION

Individuals respond to both intrinsic and extrinsic rewards. As a classroom teacher, you will encounter both all-school programs and also incentive programs within your classroom. When selecting a class incentive, select one that is both creative and also cost-effective. Allow the students some level of input into the incentive decision.

REFERENCE

Edwards, C. H. 2000. *Classroom discipline and management*. 3d ed. New York: Wiley.

WEB REFERENCE

http://express.howstuffworks.com/teachers/incentive.htm. Features stickers that the teacher can print and use with students as an incentive.

Classroom Leadership/Management

This chapter is intended for the teacher education candidate preparing to do student observations, beginning student teaching, or taking a classroom management course. The chapter is also intended for teachers currently working in the field. This information will be particularly beneficial to alternative certification candidates.

I often toss out the question in my classroom management class, "Should the name of this course be 'Classroom *Management*,' or should we change the name to 'Classroom *Leadership*'?" To be politically correct—or educationally correct— I have straddled the fence and used both topics in the title of this chapter.

Consider individuals whom you would consider "leaders" in American history. Such names may come to mind as Washington, Patton, or Sherman. The concept of a leader may have a positive or negative connotation. Historically there have been leaders who are regarded favorably or negatively today. Negative leaders had the philosophy of "my way or the highway"—even if they lived prior to highways being invented and constructed. If you prefer instead the term *management*, once again please note the name of this chapter.

William Glasser discusses the difference between boss-management and lead-management. Characteristics of the boss-management model include the following:

- The teacher or boss establishes the task and standards for the students.
- The teacher or boss usually tells, rather than shows, students how to do the work.
- The teacher or boss is the exclusive evaluator.

- When students resist, the boss uses coercion, generally in the form of punishment, to obtain compliance. (Edwards 2000: 191)

Glasser paints a grim setting for learning in the boss-management model. Employees would not want to work in this setting. Students will not want to attend school for hours per day in this setting. Glasser describes an environment more conducive to learning in the lead-management model:

- The lead-manager encourages students to discuss the quality of work they want to perform and the time constraints they wish to use.
- The lead-manager tries to fit the learning task to the skills of students.
- The lead-manager provides students with models of how they should perform and allows them to evaluate their own work.
- The lead-manager is a facilitator, establishing a nonadversarial classroom atmosphere without coercion. (Edwards 2000: 191)

For many years, I was a teacher by day and a student by night. I attended night university courses for eight years while I was a classroom teacher during the day. My dual roles helped me in many areas. It particularly helped me provide models or samples, fit learning tasks to the skills for the students, discuss the time constraints of assignments, and make learning meaningful. No student should have to complete busy work—no matter if the student is in a four-year-old program or a doctoral student! I laboriously reviewed my students before tests so that they left school with no questions unanswered. I treated my students as I wanted to be treated as a student or adult learner. Being placed in the role of the "student" made me continuously revisit my methods and practices to look for relevancy and meaning. "Because we've always done it this way" was not in my vocabulary or my mind-set.

It would be a great practice for every teacher to reflect back on their days as a student—at any level of their education. Who made the difference? Which teachers were well prepared? How did the students know? Who was an outstanding educational leader? What traits can you emulate in your classroom or in your future classroom?

Do teachers lead or manage their students? Do they incorporate a combination of leadership and management qualities into their daily life in the classroom? Some experts adamantly believe that individuals cannot manage other individuals—teachers cannot manage students. Other experts state that teachers cannot lead students. You may make your own choice as to which term you choose to use as a classroom teacher.

WHY DO STUDENTS MISBEHAVE?

An age-old question among educators is "Why do students misbehave?" Some people believe that students are bored, disengaged, or unengaged in learning. Others believe that the work is above the student's level of ability—in the realm of their frustration level. Others believe that the work is too easy— students are bored. Many educational theorists believe that it is a need for power or control. Some citizens believe that the reason is ineffective teaching, which results in ineffective learning, thus causing discipline problems. Many teacher education candidates believe that students misbehave just because they want to. Some educators believe that students misbehave at school because they have not been taught proper behavior at home. The teachers blame the parents. As you can see, much finger pointing has occurred as a result of this topic. This is a question that has baffled educators since the first schools were scattered across the eastern coast of the thirteen colonies. It is still a question seeking answers today.

Glasser believes that "what school officials say are student discipline problems are in reality school management problems" (Edwards 2000: 191). We can build on Glasser's statement to say that student discipline problems are really poor teacher management or leadership. Teachers must be prepared for a zillion things throughout each day. If they are ever *not* prepared, instruction halts and discipline problems begin.

Glasser continues with his rationale for the root of student discipline problems: "The real problem is that students struggle to resist the low-quality, standardized, fragmented curriculum that is being forced on them through coercive administrative practices" (Edwards 2000: 191). Low-quality, standardized, fragmented curriculum can be substituted for higher-level integrated curriculum in which all three learning modalities are incorporated. This learning environment created by effective teachers will promote effective learning. (See chapter 2 on "Teaching Strategies to Help Students Learn.")

A SENSE OF COMMUNITY

The topic of "building community" was mentioned previously under the characteristics of good classroom managers/leaders. This topic has been the focal point of several recent research projects. As a child, your family had close ties with your school, the neighborhood (or town) in which you lived, perhaps a religious community, perhaps an ethnic community. You and your family felt that you were a part of each group of individuals. You had close personal ties, a strong feeling of allegiance, and a desire to serve to make that "community" a better place.

Students attending school can hold similar feelings. Students bond with their teachers, school staff, administration, and volunteers. That bond, or connection, is the sense of community. "When a school meets students' basic psychological needs, students become increasingly committed to the school's norms, values, and goals. And by enlisting students in maintaining that sense of community, the school provides opportunities for students to learn skills and develop habits that will benefit them throughout their lives" (Schaps 2003: 31).

The benefits of building community have been confirmed in several research studies. Soloman et al. (2000) found that students who had a strong sense of community are more likely to be academically motivated. Schaps, Battistich, and Soloman (1997) found that these students are more likely to act ethically and altruistically. Resnick and others (1997) found that students with a strong sense of community were more likely to "avoid a number of problem behaviors, including drug use and violence." Several studies have compared students who attended elementary schools that focused on building communities preformed and those that did not. These studies have tracked the students through high school. The high school students who attended elementary schools with a community program had higher academic motivation and achievement, lower rates of violent behavior, and lower rates of heavy drinking.

As a classroom teacher, what can you do to build community? You can either work within your classroom or work as part of a schoolwide program. When your principal is on board, professional development opportunities abound, committees are formed, and parents become involved. A schoolwide effort brings the positive aspects of community building to the multitude of students attending that site.

If your principal does not wish to take this on as a schoolwide focus, you can still create a wonderful environment within your classroom. Take time at the beginning of the year to get to know each student. Keep a student data card on each student including general information as well as student interests. Build time into your days at the beginning of the year for ice-breaking activities in which students get to know each other. Using cooperative learning activities also promotes a feeling of esprit des corps among the students.

Allow parents to participate at school. Send home a letter inviting parents to volunteer their talents and/or time to help out at school. You can set this up on a weekly basis or be somewhat more creative. Consider asking parents to volunteer for a certain number of minutes per month. Individuals with a flexible or rigid schedule can still allot a designated number of minutes to offer the school, whether it's all at one visit or distributed in several shorter visits over the course of the month. Also consider offering the option of sending home something to be completed by the parent and returned to school. In all these examples, parents have the opportunity to volunteer their talents and abilities to assist their child's school.

IN SEARCH OF THE SILVER BULLET

There are several popular theories regarding classroom management and classroom discipline on the market today. Before jumping on any one of these bandwagons, know the needs of your classroom. Consider your students' expectations. Also think about the rules and policies of your school site.

No one single theory is considered the "silver bullet" of classroom management or classroom leadership. For those of you who did not grow up watching the Lone Ranger on Saturday mornings, he always saved the day with a silver bullet.

In fact, the research conducted by Emmer et al. (1980), Evertson and Emmer (1982), and Doyle (1986) has shown that effective classroom managers (and leaders) are able to blend together the best parts of different approaches. Adapt or adjust one or some of these programs to meet the needs of your classroom rather than follow a singular purist form. (Borich 2000: 381)

Research has shown that effective teachers adjust or adapt and blend the best parts of various methods to best meet the needs of their classroom and/or school site. Perhaps rather than a silver bullet to save the day, we need to create a composite bullet or a mosaic bullet—not a pure form, but rather a blend that Emmer, Evertson, and Doyle recommend—that fits the needs of our students and our classrooms. For those of you who would prefer an analogy other than a bullet, consider your management or leadership style as a quilt with a block from Skinner, a block from Canter, one from Glasser, a corner block from Gathercoal, and so on. Together, the blocks make up your method rather than a blanket consisting solely of the theory of "Jones."

THEORY AT A GLANCE

Rather than wade through a stack of theory books, consider the following information as a brief summation of eight major theorists who have written extensively on the topic of student discipline. As you read this information, imagine how you will blend these theories to best meet the needs of your classroom. Make leadership and management decisions!

- *Eric Berne and Thomas Harris.* Berne is the author of the 1967 book *I'm OK, You're OK.* The four life positions are I'm not OK—You're OK, I'm not OK—You're not OK, I'm OK—You're not OK, and I'm OK—You're OK. These are the positions students also bring into the classroom. The classroom teacher encourages students to have the I'm OK—You're OK life position. Harris originated transactional analysis, which is one method of dealing with behavioral disorders.
- *Lee Canter.* Teacher assertiveness is the key to maintaining classroom discipline. Teachers have the right to establish classroom rules and insist that students follow those rules or accept consequences.
- *Rudolf Dreikurs.* Children or students should be given a choice rather than forced to behave as directed.
- *Forrest Gathercoal.* Students may do what they want so long as it doesn't interfere with the rights of others. Teachers and students relate to one another in a democratic way. Students have responsibilities to the members of the classroom.
- *William Glasser.* Reality therapy/choice therapy places a high degree of responsibility on the students. Students determine consequences of behavior.
- *Thomas Gordon.* Gordon developed Teacher Effectiveness Training (TET), which promotes good teacher–student relationships. Students comprehend how their behavior affects others in the classroom.
- *Frederic Jones.* Teachers should teach rules and routines just like they teach any other subject (review Emmer et al.'s conclusions on effective classroom

managers). He recommends that instruction stop when discipline problems arise. This practice is the opposite strategy suggested by many educators.

- *B. F. Skinner.* The standard behavior modification model that Skinner developed encourages positive and negative reinforcement.

THEORY WEB RESOURCES

The following brief bibliography of the theorists grouped by author is intended to give you an overview of the variety of theories.

Lee Canter—Assertive Discipline (www.canter.net)

First publicized and marketed in 1976 by developer Lee Canter, assertive discipline (AD) is a well-respected and widely used program. AD focuses on the right of the teacher to define and enforce standards for student behavior. Clear expectations, rules, and a penalty system with increasingly serious sanctions are major features. (Source: www.nwrel.org/scpd/sirs/5/cu9.html.)

Curwin and Mendler—Discipline with Dignity (www.disciplineassociates.com/dwd.htm)

Discipline with Dignity presents teachers with the framework, tools, and skills for carrying out their own effective classroom management, and it furnishes administrators with information and a basis for setting schoolwide policy. Designed to allow teachers more time for instruction in a classroom environment conducive to learning, this approach also helps children develop a sense of self-esteem and gives them the encouragement and tools necessary for making responsible decisions in their lives, both inside and outside the classroom. (Source: www.disciplineassociates.com/dwd.htm.)

William Glasser—Reality Therapy (www.wglasserinst.com)

Glasser's reality therapy (RT) involves teachers helping students make positive choices by making clear the connection between student behavior and consequences. Class meetings, clearly communicated rules, and the use of plans and contracts are featured.

Positive Approach to Discipline (PAD) is based on Glasser's RT and is grounded in teachers' respect for students and instilling in them a sense of responsibility. Program components include developing and sharing clear rules, providing daily opportunities for success, and in-school suspension for noncompliant students. (Source: www.nwrel.org/scpd/sirs/5/cu9.html.)

Thomas Gordon—Teacher Effectiveness Training

Teacher Effectiveness Training (TET) differentiates between teacher-owned and student-owned problems and proposes different strategies for dealing with them. Students are taught problem-solving and negotiation techniques. (Source: www.nwrel.org/scpd/sirs/5/cu9.html.)

CONCLUSION

Whether you aspire to be a classroom manager or a classroom leader, some tricks of the trade are helpful. A general overview of classroom theories was given in this chapter as well as detailed web information. There is no single theory that best meets your needs, but rather a blend of some theories can be stirred to your specifications to best meet your students' needs.

REFERENCES

Borich, G. D. 2000. *Effective teaching methods.* 4th ed. Upper Saddle River, N.J.: Prentice Hall/Merrill.

Edwards, C. H. 2000. *Classroom discipline and management.* 3d ed. New York: Wiley.

Emmer, E. T., C. M. Evertson, and L. M. Anderson. 1980. Effective classroom management at the beginning of the school year. *Elementary School Journal* 80, no. 5: 219–31.

Resnick, M. D., P. S. Bearman, R. W. Blum, K. E. Bauman, K. M. Harris, J. Jones, J. J. Tabor, T. Beuhrin, R. E. Sieving, M. Shew, M. Ireland, L. H. Bearinger, and J. R. Udry. 1997. Protecting adolescents from harm: Findings from the National Longitudinal Study on Adolescent Health. *Journal of the American Medical Association* 278: 823–32.

Schaps, E. 2003. Creating a school community. *Educational Leadership* 60: 31–33.

Schaps, E., V. Battistich, and D. Soloman. 1997. School as a caring community: A key to character education. In *The construction of children's character: Part II. 96th yearbook of the National Society for the Study of Education,* ed. A. Molnar. Chicago: University of Chicago Press.

Solomon, D., V. Battistich, M. Watson, E. Schaps, and C. Lewis. 2000. A six-district study of educational change: Direct and mediated effects of the Child Development Project. *Social Psychology of Education* 4: 3–51.

ADDITIONAL REFERENCES
Lee Canter

Canter, L. 1994. *Assertive discipline: Teachers' plan book plus.* Vol. 1. N.p.: Lee Canter & Associates (ISBN 0939007177).

―――. 1986. *Lee Canter's assertive discipline: Administrator guide.* Lee Canter & Associates.

―――. 1992a. *Lee Canter's assertive discipline: Middle school workbook: Grades 6–8.* Rev. ed. Lee Canter & Associates.

―――. 1992b. *Lee Canter's assertive discipline: Secondary workbook: Grades 9–12.* Rev. ed. Lee Canter & Associates.

―――. 1987. *Lee Canter's assertive discipline: Teachers' plan book.* Vol. 2. Lee Canter & Associates.

―――. 1993. *Lee Canter's succeeding with difficult students: Workbook.* Lee Canter & Associates.

Curwin and Mendler

Curwin, Richard, and Allen N. Mendler. 1997. *As tough as necessary: Countering violence, aggression, and hostility in our schools.* Alexandria, Va.: Association for Supervision and Curriculum Development.

―――. 1980. *The discipline book: A complete guide to school and classroom management.* Reston, Va.: Reston.

―――. 1988. *Discipline with dignity.* Alexandria, Va.: Association for Supervision and Curriculum Development.

―――. 1983. *Taking charge in the classroom.* Rev. ed. Reston, Va.: Reston. Suggests strategies for creating consequences when students forget or do not know how to perform the behaviors agreed upon in their social contracts.

Rudolph Dreikurs

Dreikurs, Rudolf. 1998. *Maintaining sanity in the classroom: Classroom management techniques.* 2d ed. Washington, D.C.: Accelerated Development.

William Glasser

Glasser, William. 1998a. *Choice theory in the classroom.* Rev. ed. New York: HarperPerennial.

―――. 1986. *Control theory in the classroom.* New York: Perennial Library.

————. 1998b. *The quality school: Managing students without coercion.* Rev. ed. New York: HarperPerennial.

————. 1998c. *The quality school: Teacher-specific suggestions for teachers who are trying to implement the lead-management ideas of the quality school in their classrooms.* Rev. ed. New York: HarperPerennial.

Thomas Gordon

Gordon, Thomas. 1991. *Discipline that works: Promoting self-discipline in children.* New York: Plume. Offers strategies for making children more self-reliant.

————. 1987. *T.E.T.: Teacher Effectiveness Training.* New York: McKay. A guide for the classroom teacher; how to bring out the best in your students.

Frederic Jones

Jones, Frederic H. 1987a. *Positive classroom discipline.* New York: McGraw-Hill.

————. 1987b. *Positive classroom instruction.* New York: McGraw-Hill.

DAILY CLASSROOM DUTIES

MISSION STATEMENT

A classroom mission statement is a great show of unity and focus for your room. It takes very little effort after you have established your classroom rules. Any visitors to the school will quickly notice your mission statement if you post it outside your doorway. Your peers will sit up and take notice of their professional counterpart.

In my studies in educational administration, several courses discussed the importance of a mission statement as well as how to design one. As a classroom teacher, I had a class mission statement when neither the district in which I was employed nor the school site had designed one. I used my college course work to benefit classroom management. Many parents associated with the business world commented favorably about our mission statement—even parents who didn't have students in my class.

Once again, this paperwork can be designed by the teacher or completed as a group effort among class members. We simply transformed our classroom rules into a narrative paragraph form. You may also wish to add some pizzazz here or there. Use a word processor to type out your mission statement. Experiment with various fonts. Enlarge the page using the school photocopying machine or take it to a photocopy store for an ultralarge size. You may wish to have it copied onto colored paper. Laminate the final product, if you wish, and prepare to dazzle the public and receive compliments.

One final touch to a class mission statement is the addition of student signatures. If the students have been allowed input throughout the process, they will gladly and proudly sign their names to the document. Student signatures provide a win/win situation. It is a reminder to all that the class focus is not *yours*, but *ours*. It promotes a great feeling of unity or esprit de corps.

V

COMMUNICATIONS AND HUMAN RELATIONS

Children: a great way to grow people.

—Anonymous

Each major section of this book is a vital component of successful teaching. The aspect of communications and human relations is not to be glossed over or read hurriedly. Much effort and attention to detail was made when preparing this part. A classroom teacher will have problems with colleagues, administrators, staff, students, and parents in this area before any other section in this book. Make major efforts throughout each day to use your best communication and human relations skills.

Student Confidentiality

The legal issue of student confidentiality is discussed in several teacher education courses. The information in this chapter will be especially helpful when the candidate goes out into the field for observations, field experiences, or clinical practice. This chapter will also be informative to the teacher in the field today. Some districts have strict policies on student confidentiality. Others have no policy. This chapter will take a brief overview of FERPA and Falvo v. Owasso. Suggestions for "best practice" are given to help ensure the confidentiality of every student.

The topic of student confidentiality has taken a 180-degree turn over the past decade. What was considered typical classroom management for decades drastically changed due to a landmark court case. Districts went to great lengths to ensure the confidentiality of all students. The simple practice of publishing the names of honor roll students was stopped in many districts. Some districts took extreme measures to overcompensate for traditional practices of honoring or recognizing students.

The issue of student confidentiality came to the forefront of American education in 1974 with the Family Education Rights and Privacy Act (FERPA). Many educators also refer to this act as the Buckley Amendment. The term *Family* in the title shows that this law pertains to both parents and students.

This law provides two basic rights to students:

1. The right to keep records private. There are a few exceptions, such as in extreme case of emergencies or court cases.

2. The right to allow students (and their parents or legal guardian) to inspect records about themselves.

The rights of parents under FERPA cease when the student becomes eighteen years old or attends an institution of higher learning. These individuals have the right to access their own records without requesting parental permission. There are certain cases in which an underage student seeks court action to become "emancipated" from his or her own parents. In this case, the student would have the rights of a student eighteen years old.

One of the most recent major court cases to challenge FERPA occurred in Owasso, Oklahoma, and focused on peer grading of daily assignments and tests and announcing those grades to the entire class. A parent filed suit in federal court because of the practice of peer grading on daily assignments and also tests. The students in the class were calling out the grades of the papers that they graded. Kristja Falvo "said the grading practice, in which students grade other students' work and read the marks aloud, embarrassed her son and violated the federal law, which regulates the privacy of student records" (2001 Student Press Law Center, November 29, 2001, www.splc.org/newsflash.asp?id=337). In 1998, Falvo sued Owasso Public Schools, "claiming test-swapping violated a federal law that requires educational records be kept private" (http://enquirer.com/editions/2001/11/30/loc_wells_grading.html).

In the decision of the United States Court of Appeals for the Tenth Circuit in *Falvo v. Owasso Independent School District No. 1-0011*, the court concluded that the practice of having students exchange papers and grade those papers and the practice of having students call out their grades in class in the presence of other students violated FERPA. The impact of *Falvo* hit hard throughout the American educational system. Administrators and boards of education reexamined their practices and policies. The phrase "because we've always done it this way" was tossed out the window. Districts across the country closely examined their confidentiality policies.

Considerable time passed, but eventually the U.S. Supreme Court reviewed *Falvo v. Owasso*. The Supreme Court *unanimously* voted to overturn the Court of Appeals decision. They rejected the finding that FERPA was violated when students exchanged papers, graded those papers, and called out the grades in class in the presence of other students.

A unanimous decision by the Supreme Court is not to be second-guessed.

In the wake of this ruling, the KASB legal department recommends that boards and administrators consider the educational implications of peer grading before returning to this practice. It is up to the school district to decide the best educational practice for the students of the district. What is clear from this decision is that, for now, the practice of peer grading is an educational technique that is not prohibited by FERPA. (www .accesskansas.org/kasb.falvo.html)

Educators can establish "best practice" policies in which districts or sites establish agendas to preserve the integrity of the classroom and ensure the confidentiality of each student.

BEST-PRACTICE SUGGESTIONS
As an educator, please consider the following guidelines:

- Keep your students' abilities and grades confidential.
- Do not allow a parent volunteer, student assistant, or student aide to grade papers or enter grades in the grade book. *Exception:* An exception would be a teacher education candidate (student teacher, clinical practitioner, or student intern) assigned to your classroom from an area university. This individual will have the opportunity to learn all aspects of the teaching process. A student teacher is a university teacher education major. A student assistant or student aide is a student from within your district.
- Do not allow a parent or guardian to see the grade book. When such individuals view this book, they are viewing *all* the students' grades.
- Never allow children to call out or say another child's grades aloud.
- Refrain from putting up corrected work for public viewing (i.e., on the bulletin board). Consider displaying students' work that has a *separate* grading rubric, checklist, or rating scale, which is concealed from view. (See chapter 13 for further information on rubrics, checklists, and rating scales.) Do not display any material that shows a letter grade, numerical grade, or teacher comments.
- Stop any practice of allowing students to hand out graded papers to other students. Another practice to avoid is placing graded papers in a stack, box,

or basket and having students go through the papers to retrieve their own graded paper. They will see everyone's grades until they find their paper.

■ Discontinue any practice of having students exchange papers for the purpose of grading those papers and assigning grades to them.

■ Ensure that grade books, graded papers or projects, computerized grading programs, e-mail, or similar electronic transmissions concerning student grades and other material from which students or others could determine a particular student's grade are treated as confidential records.

One possible solution to returning corrected work is to ask students to fold the paper (either vertically or horizontally) in half before they turn it in. Ask them to write their name on the outside of the folded paper. You can make any corrections on the paper and even write a grade on it. When it is refolded, no one can see the comments or grade. To avoid any problems, please ask your building principal about the school's policy regarding returning corrected student papers.

WEB REFERENCES

To read the documentation on *Falvo v. Owasso* and the issue of peer grading, see the following web addresses:

www.caselaw.lp.findlaw.com/cgi-bin/getcase.pl?court=10th&navby=case&no=
    995130

www.accesskansas.org/kasb/falvo.html

www.utea.org/docs/news/ueaAction/dec01/opinion/StudentPrivacy&Courts,htm

www.splc.org/newsflash.asp?id=337

http://clickit.go2net.com/search?cid=239171&site=srch&area=srch.noncomm
    .google&shape=textlink&cp=dogpile&rawto=http://www.nsea.org/voice/
    VoiceGradingPapers.pdf

http://enquirer.com/editions/2001/11/30/loc_wells_grading.html

www.educationworld.com/a_issues/issues279.shtml

Web information regarding FERPA include the following sources:

www.cpsr.org/cpsr/privacy/ssn/ferpa.buckley.html

www.ed.gov/offices/OM/fpco/ferparegs.html

20

Conferences

This chapter is targeted for all three intended readerships. The teacher education candidate will learn basics and beyond for conferences. When this topic arises in your teacher preparation courses, you will have information to share with your fellow students (who have not read this book). For those teaching in the field, you can begin now taking notes and deciding which pearls of wisdom shared in this chapter will best meet your needs. Look carefully at the visual examples. You can easily adapt these to best fit your needs.

This chapter offers Technology Excursion Trips. Steps are given to use technology to assist you in preparation for conferences.

Conferences are like any major holiday, such as Thanksgiving, Christmas, or Hanukah. You know the day is coming; thus, you begin to prepare weeks in advance for the big event. Also like major holidays, conferences involve several individuals rather than just you. Conferences today in public and private schools include the classroom teacher as well as the parent(s) or custodial guardian. Other professionals who might be involved in conferences include the school counselor, other teachers who also work with the student throughout the day or week, and specialty teachers. A final individual that is now involved in many conferences is the student—in student-led conferences.

Conference day is the time that parents, grandparents, and guardians come to visit confidentially with you about the individual student's progress. Successful conferences do not *just happen*. Success is the end result or the reward for strategic preparation prior to the conferences, professional techniques during the conference, and follow-up and follow-through after the conferences.

There is no singular design or blueprint for successful conferences. I believe that a key is preparedness. Take the proactive position and prepare your classroom, your handouts, your students' current academic standing, and set your conference goals. You will have different goals with each visitor.

Design your room so that you have a table surrounded with chairs for adults. Too often visitors at elementary schools have no alternative but to sit in student-sized chairs. Arrange your conference area so that the visitors will have adult-sized chairs and also be able to view the documents you plan to show. Realize in advance that you need to be able to read upside down or have the chairs arranged so that everyone can see the papers from the same perspective. Extra attention to details prior to the arrival of the guests will be a major asset when it's "show time."

Use air freshener, carpet freshener, potpourri—anything to help the classroom smell divine. Most schools frown on burning a scented candle for the obvious fire hazard reasons. Find some way to make the room smell fresh.

Prior to the arrival of the guests, dust and clean every inch of the classroom. Notify the custodian if all lights are not working. Also notify your custodian about any stained ceiling tiles (which will be a sure sign of a leaking roof). Parents are also taxpayers. They expect a clean and well-organized school.

One year I had a meeting to attend the afternoon prior to parent conferences. The substitute teacher used furniture wax, rather than the household cleaner that I laid out, to clean the students' desks. (Yes, it *was* written specifically in the substitute plans!) The desks glimmered and smelled sensational. None of the parents ever knew my problem. I did, however, have to scrub for days to get that wax film off the desktops. In any event, we achieved our goal of clean desks.

Obviously the school has some manner in which parents select a time slot for conferences. Use a word processor to design a short form to be sent home to remind/confirm the date and time of the conference. This will take a short amount of your time, but it will show the parent your sincerity and desire to meet with them. Figure 20.1 is an example of a form that could be used.

A week or two prior to conference day, begin saving samples of student papers. Have a file folder for each student. When you receive a schedule of par-

FIGURE 20.1
Sample conference template

XYZ Public Schools

Parent's name _____ Student's name _____
Our parent-teacher conferences will be held at Jones Elementary School on Friday,
October 18. Your conference time is at _____. I look forward to meeting you.

Thank you,
John Doe

---

ents coming, put the file folders in a stack with the papers of the first visiting
parent's child on top. Just take the folder off the top during the conference and
discuss the work. Before the parent leaves, give him or her the papers. Parents
will be impressed with your organization. This will also give you credibility in
the eyes of the parent, which is much needed for any teacher. The parent will
have a visual verification of the child's progress. If you are using a behavior
chart, discuss it at the conference also.

Another task to take care of a week or two prior to conferences is the special needs of the parents. If you need a translator for an LEP/ESL parent, ask
your administrator or counselor for that assistance at a specific time on a specific date. If the parent is hearing impaired, prepare in advance for a
"signer"—a sign language specialist—to be present. If any parents are visually
or physically impaired, will they need assistance locating the room? Would it
be easier for you to change the location of the conference for easier access? Just
as professionals make every effort to meet the needs of all students, we also
make every possible effort to assist parents with special or unique needs. Plan
ahead.

If your conferences are timed, be certain that the parents know the time
frame in advance of their visit. Consider using an egg timer to ensure that you
do not go over your time limit. Set it for three or four minutes less than your
time limit. This will allow you time to thank the parent for coming, give a professional handshake, and greet the next parent waiting for the conference. Just
as we all hate to be kept waiting for an appointment, so do parents. Be prompt
with your conferences.

I once sat for an hour to see my son's teacher on conference day. Yes, I had
a scheduled appointment. As my mental frustration monitor soared to the

"intolerable chaos" level, I began to wonder whether she ran her classroom in the same haphazard fashion she conducted her conferences. Parents will begin to "connect the dots" as they form a professional impression of you. Provide them with a great set of experiences and impressions so that they will create an outstanding profile of you.

One of my colleagues always tells me, "It doesn't matter what you say—it's how good you look that counts." Regarding parent conferences, both areas—looks and content of your conference—matter. Dress professionally. Jeans and a sweatshirt are great for a trip to the grocery store, but dress professionally to meet your students' parents. Also be prepared to be informative and helpful.

Word of caution: Never ever discuss another student's progress or behavior during conferences. Maintain *every* child's confidentiality—it's not only considered professional, it's also the law. (See "Student Confidentiality" discussed in the prior chapter.)

For one reason or another, I often went to students' homes to visit with their parents. I quickly picked up on the inadequate feeling of "being on someone else's turf." Parents can feel the same way when they come to school for a visit with the teacher. The parents have come to your "turf." Make every effort to be gracious and hospitable to all parents, grandparents, or guardians who have taken the time and made the effort to visit your school.

As a classroom teacher, you may not be the only individual having a conference with the parents. In a team teaching situation, all teachers generally will meet (as a team) with parents. In a departmentalized setting, often all the teachers involved will meet with the parents. At the middle school and high school levels, often a group of teachers within a "pod" or "quad" will meet with parents. Be prepared to be an equal contributor to the conference if you are part of a team.

Here is a list of suggestions for a professional parent–teacher conference. Only a professional educator will take the time and make the effort to go the extra mile before, during, and after the conference.

- Welcome the parent into the conference with a professional handshake. Thank him or her in advance for coming.

- Introduce other individuals present if this is a team meeting. Consider wearing name tags for the entire day of conferences. This will be helpful to parents.
- Not only speak professionally but also listen intently. Parents can shed light on many issues that will assist you as the child's teacher. Parents also like to be valued and heard.
- Be aware of your body language. It speaks volumes.
- Be prepared with written or verbal suggestions of ways in which the child can improve. For example, you might encourage the parent to take the student to the local library for special events to promote reading. You could provide them with a handout from the library with dates and times. Perhaps your school is having a special day camp over the winter holidays for children. You might give the parents flyer about the camp—not as an advertisement but rather as a form of assistance if they work outside the home.
- If you use a computerized grading system, utilize this at conference time. Have printouts available of the present or past grading period, depending on the time of the conference. Know where the student stands academically at this point in time also.
- Ask the powerful, mighty, and all-important question "Are you receiving the communications that we are sending home?" If so, rejoice and be glad. If not, design a game plan that will ensure clear and open communication lines with the home.
- Prepare a set of handouts for the parents in advance. Keep in mind that your familiar world of school each day is foreign to most parents. Work with the families to build a bridge of communication and cooperation between home and school. Consider carefully what information would be helpful to parents at your school in your district. Some things you might wish to include are the following:

  The most recent copy of the school newsletter

  Any form of printed class communications you have recently created, such as a weekly or monthly calendar

  The address of your school's website

  Your e-mail address at school

  If the district has an annual calendar on a single sheet of paper, make copies to distribute to all the parents.

✗ **Technology Excursion Trip** *You may wish to create your own calendar for one month. Open Word. Go to File, then New. You will find templates. The newer Word programs will have a group of "Other Documents." You will find a template to create a monthly calendar and also be able to type in specific information for special things happening in your school or in your classroom.*

Prepare a calendar of future events to give with your set of handouts. Perhaps a schoolwide science fair is coming in a few weeks, or your school will have an assembly featuring Native American dancers next month. Mark the dates, times, and events on the calendar. Verbally or in written form invite parents to come to school and share these events with their child.

✗ **Technology Excursion Trip** *If you are computer-savvy, make your own business cards that include your school phone number, e-mail address, and school web page address. Open Word, go to Tools, and scroll down to Labels and Envelopes. Find "Business Cards." Create your own personalized card using the template. You can either print it out on the photocopying paper at the school or print it out on business card sheets. Most office supply stores will allow you to buy only the number of business card sheets you need, rather than purchasing a large package of them. Buy what you need and pay the $0.05 or $0.06 per sheet to have the cards photocopied. Your home printer may be able to print them out also. The sheets are perforated so that they easily break apart. Imagine how impressed your visitors will be to receive a business card from their child's teacher.*

- Provide plain paper from the copy machine and a pen or pencil for the parent to take notes. You also have paper and a pencil to take notes. Please use a separate sheet of paper for each student! Both you and the parent will have written documentation of the meeting, goals, objectives, suggestions, and so forth. You may wish to type out a simple conference form using the word processor to use. Samples appear later in the figures.

- Impress on the parent your sincere appreciation for their support, cooperation, and assistance since the beginning of school. Appreciation is a two-way street. You have to give it to get it.

- If some form of follow-up is needed, please set a date or a week in which you will be contacting the parent. Will the follow-up be by phone, e-mail, or a note sent home? Mutually decide on your mode of communication.

- Always conclude all conferences by asking the parents if they have any additional questions. Take time to answer everything before they leave.

- Conclude the conference with a professional handshake and sincere thank you.

Figure 20.2 is a generic example of a conference form that could be used by any teacher in the XYZ School District at any grade level. Figure 20.3 is a more specific example of a form that can be created. This example has an agenda to provide specific information to the teacher. Figure 20.4 is an example designed for a secondary teacher that has a variety of teaching responsibilities. This example is for a Social Studies teacher. The teacher can circle the appropriate course and section for the student. Having over a hundred students each day, this extra effort will be helpful both during and after the conference. Figure 20.5 illustrates a completed form.

Taking the time to document your conference information will be a major asset to you. Written documentation is a great solution when the parent contacts your administrator about a problem. You have documentation that will give you credibility. Rather than trying to remember something from one of thirty-nine conferences you conducted four weeks ago, you will have important details written down. The extra effort you make during conferences will pay off huge dividends later in the year.

STUDENT-LED CONFERENCES
The traditional parent–teacher conference has changed over the years, extending to grandparents caring for their grandchildren and also legal

FIGURE 20.2
Generic conference template

XYZ Public Schools—Parent–Teacher Conference

October 18, 2____
Student's name:
Individual representing student:
Goals:

Follow-up date: Mode of communication:
Follow-up purpose:

FIGURE 20.3
Parent–teacher conference template

```
XYZ Public Schools—Parent–Teacher Conference

October 18, 2____
Student's name:
Individual representing student:
Teacher concerns:

Parent concerns:

Goals:


Is parent receiving communications?          Y          N
Does parent have access to e-mail?           Y          N
Phone calls should be                        at home    at work
Does parent have time to volunteer at school?  Y        N


Follow-up date:               Mode of communication:
Follow-up purpose:
```

FIGURE 20.4
Secondary social studies conference form

```
XYZ Public Schools—Parent–Teacher Conference

Student is in:   Civics    U.S. History       Government       Geography

Student is in:   1st hour   2d hour   3d hour   4th hour   5th hour   6th hour
October 18, 2____
Student's name:
Individual representing student:
Teacher concerns:
Goals:



Follow-up date:               Mode of communication:
Follow-up purpose:
```

FIGURE 20.5
Completed social studies conference form

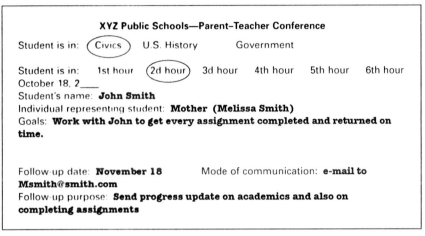

guardians overseeing children's lives. Another person who has been included in these conferences in recent years is the student. Some districts have conferences in which the student leads the conference. The student shows the parents the "work" that has been saved. The student gives her or his perspective on the project or assignment.

My first impression of student-led conferences was to associate the concept with students at the middle or high school level. I learned that student-led conferences have no age level. Do not underestimate primary students because they have limited reading and/or writing abilities. They can, to use verbs from Bloom's Synthesis and Evaluation levels of the taxonomy, conclude, contrast, critique, criticize, judge, justify, interpret, organize, and summarize.

We invited three guest speakers to visit my evaluations and measurements classroom to share their experiences with student-led conferences. Two were primary team teachers. The third speaker was a kindergarten student who captivated the teacher education candidates with her perspective of student-led conferences. Yes, she *was* cute, but she also relayed firsthand experiences that were invaluable to the future teachers in the audience.

Student-led conferences create a win/win situation. The student is the focus and purpose of the conference in the first place. Educators in all corners of the globe will agree that students need to accept more responsibility. Give it to them in this realm. An old proverb states, "We gain power when we give it away." You can gain the trust and respect of your students and parents by successfully using this technique.

Student-led conferences have many positive aspects. Your parent attendance percentage will improve with student-led conferences. The student will make every effort to have his or her parent there. The student and parent can also come and leave together. You can be certain that the student's locker and desk will be in A+ condition also. According to Seliner and Bushey (1997), your students will play a more active role in their learning, take more ownership of their work, and assume responsibility for how productive they have— or have not—been.

Before conducting student-led conferences, please discuss this plan with your administrator. Visit with your students about the goals or purposes of the conference. Allow them to see in advance all the "work" that you will be giving to their parents. Make major efforts to alleviate any anxiety they may have. Also decide whether the conferences are to be timed, and, if so, stress the importance of staying within that time boundary.

Seliner and Bushey (1997), who both work with fifth-grade students, have parent–teacher conferences in the fall in order for both parties to get to know each other. In the spring they have student-led conferences. Among the list of things to do prior to conferences, the authors stress to have a checklist for the students to make sure that they cover specific items and also to have practice sessions. Seliner and Bushey role-play with the students. One teacher plays the part of the student conducting the conference, and a student volunteer plays the part of the parent. This provides a modeling example for the student, followed by a question-and-answer session so that the students thoroughly understand their role.

Consider ending the student-led conference with the student verbally sharing his or her goals for the next quarter or to be achieved by the end of the present quarter. For example, "Before the end of the quarter, I hope to raise my math grade from a B+ to an A," or "Next quarter I hope to have every assignment turned in on time." The last thing everyone will hear before adjourning is a positive statement that has been thoughtfully considered by the student. The conference will thus end in an optimistic fashion.

Seliner and Bushey (1997) have parents complete a survey sheet for feedback. Their parental response was "overwhelmingly positive." You can design a standard survey sheet using the word processor. You might also consider designing a feedback sheet for the students to complete as well. If your administrator inquires about the successes of your student-led conferences, you will have both parental and student evaluations for verification.

As a new teacher to the district, ask in advance about conferences. Just as you would prepare the students in advance for student-led conferences, also make major efforts to relieve *your* anxieties. If you fail to plan, you plan to fail.

CONCLUSION

Conferences are a great opportunity to improve communication between school and home. Successful conferences do not just happen. They are the harvest of much preparation and advance work on the teacher's part.

Special consideration is taken to make the parents, grandparents, foster parents, or other adult caregivers as welcome as possible. By preparing in advance, adaptations can be made to meet any special needs the visitors may have.

Documentation is a key element to successful conferences. Proper documentation helps the teacher maintain proper goals and aspirations for each student. Proper documentation can also be a great resource if a parent problem should arise in the future.

When the parents visit schools, the school or the teacher should be ready with calendars, newsletters, any and all forms of handouts to maximize human relations, and communications skills.

REFERENCES

Austin, T. 1994. *Changing the view: Student-led parent conferences.* New York: Heinemann. (To order, call [800] 793-2154.)

Benson, B., and S. Barnett. 1998. Student-led conferences using showcase portfolios. New York: Corwin.

Cleland, J. V. 1999. We-can charts: Building blocks for student-led conferences. *Reading Teacher* 52, no. 6: 588–95.

Conderman, G., P. Ikan, and R. Hatcher. 2000. Student-led conferences in inclusive settings. *Intervention in School and Clinic* 36, no. 1 (September): 22–26.

Guyton, J., and L. Fielstein. 1989. Student-led parent conferences: A model for teaching responsibility. *Elementary School Guidance and Counseling* 24, no. 2 (December): 169–72.

Hackmann, D., J. Kennworthy, and S. Nibbelink. 1998. Student empowerment through student-led conferences. *Middle School* 300, no. 1: 35–39.

Le Countryman, L., and M. Schroeder. 1996. When students lead parent–teacher conferences. *Educational Leadership* 53, no. 7: 64–68.

Lenski, S. 1996. Honoring student self-evaluation in the classroom community. *Primary Voices K–6* 4, no. 2 (April): 24–32.

Picciotto, L. P. 1996. *Student-led parent conferences.* New York: Scholastic. (To order, call [800] 724-6527.)

Santa, C. 1995. Assessment: Students lead their own parent conferences. *Teaching Pre-K–8* 25, no. 7 (April): 92, 94.

Seliner, B., and J. Bushey. 1997. Student-led parent conferences. *Learning* 26, no. 3 (November–December): 44–49.

Shannon, K. 1997. Student-led conferences: A twist on tradition. *Schools in the Middle* 6, no. 3 (January-February): 47–49.

21

Behavior Charts

This chapter is designed primarily for the alternative certification candidate and the teacher who has come from a traditional teacher education background— teachers in the field. The examples in this chapter were created using Microsoft Word. You can create similar charts to meet the needs of your students or classroom.

The teacher education candidate will see the need for documentation of student behavior when making classroom observations, completing internships, or conducting student teaching/clinical practice.

Some schools have a behavior sheet or chart that goes home with the student every week. This chart is then signed by the parents and returned to school by a designated day. Behavior charts are a great way for parents to know how their children are behaving at school. They can also provide feedback on areas that are improving or need to improve. Behavior charts are also weekly documentation (documentation, documentation) on the student's actions. They provide a source of documentation when behavioral referrals are made to the administration office.

If your school does not have a prepared behavior chart, you might want to construct one yourself. Consider a checklist form(see chapter 12). Decide on your indicators and keep the number small. Possible indicators could be "Works well with classmates" or "Comes prepared for class." The former is *subjective* and the latter is *objective*. Objective indicators allow little room for debate or dispute. You might want your indicators to come straight from your classroom rules. How will you measure these indicators? You may choose to use "Improving," "Great," and "Needs Improvement" or *I*, *G*, or *N* in the appropriate spaces. Perhaps you have stamps in which you could use symbols as indicators. Add an indicator that shows that you did not observe a behavior, due to your absence, the child's absence, or another reason. Create a behavior chart for each week, quarter, or grading period.

When designing a behavior chart, the most important rule is "Keep it simple." Simplicity in design for you, the student, and the parents will help all parties understand how things are going. The basic design can run horizontally or vertically. You as the creator have the choice.

The chart in table 21.1 is designed for John Smith for a single week. This chart could be sent home each week on the day that all communications go home to parents. There is a space for the parent to sign and date. There is also a space for you to note when the chart was returned. You could use a stamp with the date to give you assistance. The final space is for parental comments.

You may find as a classroom teacher that some children are bright and brilliant in the morning but falter as the afternoon progresses. Consider subdividing your behavior chart for morning and afternoon. The advantage to you as a classroom teacher is that you will have documentation (documentation,

Table 21.1.   Behavior Chart for John Smith for One Week

John Smith October 1–5	Mon.	Tues.	Wed.	Thurs.	Fri.
Returns communications from home	I	X	X	X	X
Returns completed assignments	G	G	G	G	G
Has necessary supplies	G	G	G	G	G
Follows verbal and written directions	G	G	G	G	G
Works independently/self-motivated	I	G	G	I	G
Shares ideas with the class	I	I	I	I	I
Listens to others	G	G	G	G	G
Keeps hands, feet, objects to himself	G	G	G	G	G

G – Good   N – Needs to Improve   I = Improving   X   Did not observe
Parental signature   Date   Date returned
Comments:

documentation) that this particular student is falling behind after lunch in one or more specific areas. A conference with the parent will assist you in learning the cause of this problem, which could be one of many factors. Having a chart similar to the one in table 21.2 will give you credibility with the parent. You can also show this information to your school counselor or principal for further advice. This chart shows that John Smith is having difficulties after lunch.

I worked very hard to get to know my students as well as possible at the beginning of each school year. I had some students who developed a pattern over many weeks in which they were not up to par on Tuesday mornings. They were very quiet, slow, sluggish, and just not their usual selves. I finally realized

Table 21.2.   Morning and Afternoon Behavior Chart for John Smith for One Week

John Smith October 1–5	Mon.	Tues.	Wed.	Thurs.	Fri.
Returns communications from home	G	X	X	X	X
Returns completed assignments	G	G	G	G	G
Has necessary supplies	G	G	G	G	G
A.M.: Follows verbal and written directions	G	G	G	G	G
P.M.: Follows verbal and written directions	N	I	I	N	I
A.M.: Works independently/ self-motivated	G	G	G	G	G
P.M.: Works independently/ self-motivated	N	N	N	I	N
A.M.: Shares ideas verbally with class	G	G	G	G	G
P.M.: Shares ideas verbally with class	N	I	N	I	N
A.M.: Listens well to the ideas of others	G	G	G	G	G
P.M.: Listens well to the ideas of others	N	N	I	N	I
A.M.: Keeps hands, feet, objects to himself	G	G	G	G	G
P.M.: Keeps hands, feet, objects to himself	N	N	N	N	N

G Good	I = Improving	N Needs improvement	X = Did not observe

Parental signature	**Date**	**Date returned**

Comments:

in casual conversation that they were staying up till the wee hours to watch the end of *Monday Night Football.* If this cycle had started in the middle of the year, I would have been very concerned. Because I was still getting to know my students, I didn't catch the pattern immediately. A behavior chart designed like the one presented earlier would have documented their behavior pattern over the week's span. It would have obvious to see.

Some districts encourage teachers to record a behavior chart on a monthly basis. Table 21.3 shows John Smith's chart for February. This chart is kept on a daily basis. The teacher can make it as simple or as complex as is needed. The chart will be sent home for a signature when the month is completed.

Table 21.3.   Behavior Chart for John Smith for One Month

John Smith **FEBRUARY**				
Feb. 1 1 G 2 I 3 G	Feb. 2 1 G 2 I 3 G	Feb. 3 1 G 2 I 3 G	Feb. 4 1 G 2 I 3 G	Feb. 5 1 X 2 X 3 X
Feb. 8 1 2 3	Feb. 9 1 2 3	Feb. 10 1 2 3	Feb. 11 1 2 3	Feb. 12 1 2 3
Feb. 15 1 2 3	Feb. 16 1 2 3	Feb. 17 1 2 3	Feb. 18 1 2 3	Feb. 19 1 2 3
Feb. 22 1 2 3	Feb. 23 1 2 3	Feb. 24 1 2 3	Feb. 25 1 2 3	Feb. 26 1 2 3

1 = Returns assignments on time   G = Good   N = Needs improvement

2 = Works independently/self-motivated   I = Improving   X = Did not observe

3 = Follows verbal and written directions

Parental signature _____ Date _____

Date returned _____

After you have established the design of your behavior chart, consider where this chart will be kept. A simple student folder with a three-hole holder in the center and pockets on each side would be an excellent choice. You may have access to another system through your district or the generosity of parents that would meet your needs.

Run off sets of the behavior chart for each student. Three-hole-punch the sets, or ask a student or parent helper to complete this task. As a penmanship lesson or as a "following directions" lesson, have the students write their names on each chart. Ask them to write their names on the outside cover of the folder. You can use a stamp for the dates or write them on the board and ask students to copy them onto each page.

The final step for you is to decide where the folders will be kept during the week. Use a specific shelf or a basket to hold each student's behavior charts. Be certain that the students know where they are to be kept.

Also make a note in your substitute folder about where they are kept. Decide in advance if you wish for the substitute to mark the behaviors or to leave the marking to you. Write this information in your substitute folder.

As with any innovation you want to try with your students, discuss this with your principal and get approval before proceeding. Use your talents to create an effective behavior chart that will both keep the parents informed and also provide documentation, documentation, documentation for you. Behavior charts turn to gold when used in a parent conference or when a child is referred to the principal for a behavior problem. You will have specific dates and specific behaviors that you can pinpoint in a moment's notice rather than trying to rely on your memory for such details. A small amount of effort on your part will provide a finely detailed profile of the child's behavior over time. A chart designed by the day or even the morning and afternoons will provide even finer detail to the behavior composite.

COMMUNICATIONS AND HUMAN RELATIONS

PHONING HOME

The beginning of school is a great time for teachers to get to know their students and also their students' parents. Take the first couple of weeks of school to call each set of parents. If you have twenty students, that's two families per day, and you're finished in two weeks. If you have many students at the secondary level, divide the names among several teachers who mutually work with the students. If and/or when you need to call again, they will be much more receptive to your call.

Keep your initial phone call very brief and cheerful. Decide in advance on one or two points you wish to make. One could be the day of the week you will be sending home communications and papers. Perhaps you would like to give the school's website information to the parent. You might want to share the date and time of Parents' Night when they can come to school.

Consider the privacy issue. You may not be in a private place to discuss confidential matters nor may the parent. Therefore, keep this introductory phone call brief and to the point.

Consider also the medium in which you are communicating. As a classroom teacher, you will have cell phone numbers, pager numbers, beeper numbers, e-mail addresses, and also home and office phone numbers. If you choose to make contact during the day, be sensitive to the parent you are contacting. Obviously, some of these choices will not give you direct immediate contact with the parent. You will be required to wait and follow through on your initial contact. Using a cell phone, work phone, or home phone may be your best option. Time is a precious commodity for both teachers and parents.

Important note: If you call the parents from your home, remember that technology has made great advancements. Due to caller ID, individuals will know your phone number henceforth and forever more or, as we like to say in Oklahoma, "as long as the grass grows and the rivers flow." Contact your phone company to see how you can block out your phone number from being read on caller IDs.

SENDING HOME CORRECTED WORK

Albert Einstein has been quoted as saying, "God never threw dice." I translate this to mean that there was great effort to create order and structure in the universe. As a professional, you will also not "throw dice." You will have order and structure in your daily classroom life. One way is to create a consistent pattern when sending home communications and corrected work.

Some teachers like to send home all work from the week on the same day each week. These are teachers who do not "throw dice." Idealistically thinking, Friday would be the optimum day. Realistically, however, Friday has some drawbacks. Consider your spelling tests. You will have to correct every test, record it in the grade book, and return it to the student before they leave on Friday. That is difficult, especially if you have lunch duty responsibilities on Fridays. Also consider that many students do not go home on Fridays. Due to custody arrangements, they may go to another home after school. The custodial parent will not see the schoolwork every week.

For several years I sent home a class calendar with all events and major assignments/tests marked for the next week on Friday. I had to have all my lesson plans made out Thursday night *and* type my calendar Thursday evening. I did not teach spelling, so I had no problem there. My partner who did teach spelling sent home her calendar and work on Monday night. She had all weekend to correct the spelling tests and other work and plan for the following week. Each situation has its advantages and disadvantages. Look closely at your classroom and professional needs and select the day that is best for all of you.

The parents are the most important ingredients in the recipe for student success. By taking some time to educate parents about your routine, they will be looking for work or a class calendar on a specific day. Be consistent, and don't roll dice at school!

COMMUNICATIONS

Teaching is not an island. Teaching is a team effort or a team approach. Many individuals are involved in educating students. One or two of the most important individuals are the student's parents, custodial grandparents, or guardians. Every such person appreciates communication with the school. Many school sites prepare a general newsletter monthly. Professionals make every effort to keep parents up to date on their classroom activities more often than monthly.

As an elementary teacher, I sent home a class calendar weekly. A weekly parent update can be as detailed or general as you wish. Using the word processor, you can make a template and then type or handwrite the information. Presented here is a sample of a calendar that would be sent home with the students the Friday *before* Monday, April 3. Parents and students will know at a glance what is coming up for the following week.

	Mrs. Smith's Fifth-Grade Class Calendar
Monday April 3	Begin new chapter in social studies—chapter 16, "America Moves West" Spelling bonus words for week: vertebrate, invertebrate, mollusk, echinoderm
Tuesday April 4	
Wednesday April 5	Science exam covering chapter 12, "Invertebrates"; study questions were sent home Friday, March 29
Thursday April 6	Assembly in the gym—Freddie the Friendly Firehouse Clown, 10:00 A.M. Parents and family are invited.
Friday April 7	Spelling test—chapter 38 Calendar for following week, corrected papers, and science test go home tonight.

As a university supervisor for first-year teachers, I always visit
with my teachers about the methods of communication they are
using. One teacher proudly told me about a class calendar that
she sent home every week. I was very surprised to learn as the
conversation proceeded that she sent home a calendar of things
that had *already occurred* rather than a calendar of things to
come. In other words, she was preparing a past-tense calendar
rather than a calendar in the future tense. After our conversation,
her calendar changed tenses. It is fruitless to prepare a list of past
events when the same time, effort, and paper usage can be put
into preparing a useful preview of the upcoming events in your
classroom or at your school.

One thing to avoid putting into print on a calendar or newsletter
is any student's first and last name. I avoided this for security
reasons. If a new student enrolled in the middle of the year, I
would include in the calendar the following: "We wish to welcome Susan to our classroom." Susan's last name or former
school location were not put into print. I also did not put students' last names on the lockers. Any individual could walk
down our halls and read the students' names. For the students'
security, I did not put last names on anything that could be
viewed by the public. I also avoided name tags on field trips. Although this would have been helpful to parent helpers and
school personnel on the trip, it could also have posed potential
danger to the students.

I used enormous amounts of paper and was never quite sure how
many of these calendars and other communications actually
made it home. Being a professional in the age of technology, consider sending e-mails to your parents.

A middle school teacher in Skiatook, Oklahoma, has made this a
practice. When the students enroll, the Skiatook district asks parents to write their e-mail addresses on the enrollment form. The
teachers have access to this information. One individual teaches

three "block sections" of mathematics and science. She has the same lesson plans for all three sections. This teacher sends the parents a weekly update to notify them on chapters or topics they are studying, test dates, project due dates, and so forth. She will also send out an e-mail requesting supplies needed for experiments such as boxes of corn starch or plastic cups.

This story is another example of a win/win situation. The teacher simply types the message and then sends it to everyone on the e-mail list. If she chose the class calendar route, she would have to type out the message, find a photocopy machine and make the copies, and then distribute to all students and pray that the middle school students would take them home. (Dream on!) The e-mail approach is a sure-fire way of knowing that the messages are reaching the parents. Imagine the time saved by using an e-mail system rather than personally calling each parent or sending home an informative written communication.

If you choose this approach, parents will be well informed and appreciative. Your administrator will have fewer complaints from your parents. Your professionalism will pay off in many ways. The beauty of informative e-mails is that it takes so little effort on the part of the teacher.

I advise you to set up "Netiquette guidelines" for your parents so that you won't have fifty to a hundred responses to your e-mail every week. Your time is valuable. Some Netiquette guidelines you might consider for parents include the following:

- Keep the communication short.
- If it's urgent, call rather than e-mail.
- Ask the parents to focus on their child, rather than e-mail information about other children.
- The teacher's response may not be immediate.

You may be fortunate enough to be employed in a district that has already established e-mail guidelines for parents and teachers. If not, take the initiative and establish your own before a problem raises its ugly head. Again, if you fail to plan, you plan to fail. Professionals plan ahead.

A recent story in *Family PC* magazine cited as an example the Northshore School District in Bothell, Washington. Teachers there were feeling so overwhelmed by parent e-mail that the teachers' union initiated a discussion of the district's e-mail behavior during contract negotiations last spring.

The message is clear: Simply dumping technology into teacher's laps isn't going to work. It will require planning, careful integration, and cooperation among parents, teachers, and school administrators.

Whether you send a weekly newsletter or calendar or informative e-mails, remember that you still will not be reaching 100 percent of the parents. Not all parents will have access to e-mails. Not all children are responsible for delivering newsletters or calendars. The important element is that you have made the effort to communicate with the parents.

Take one final step: Keep a file or disk with all your communications. You will have documentation, documentation, documentation of your efforts. You can include this information in an end-of-the-year report or in your professional portfolio. A future employer will be impressed with both your efforts and your excellent ability to maintain documentation. Most important, when a problem arises, you have made a concerned effort to keep the parents updated on current events. Your attention to detail will pay off with the parents and with your administrator. Once again, some additional time and effort will help you in your journey from teacher to professional.

REFERENCE

Kemper, E., and M. Ivey. 2001. E-mail can be made to benefit teachers. *Tulsa World*, May 7, sec. D, 4.

VI

THE JOURNEY FROM TEACHER TO PROFESSIONAL

The mediocre teacher tells. The good teacher explains. The superior teacher demonstrates. The great teacher inspires.

—*William Arthur Ward*

Much have I learned from my teachers, more from my colleagues, but most from my students.

—*Talmud*

There is no more noble profession than teaching. A great teacher is a great artist, but his medium is not canvas, but the human soul.

—*Anonymous*

Part VI is designed as an overview for the teacher education candidate. Alternative certification teachers will benefit from both the general and specific aspects of this section. The teacher who came through the traditional teacher education route will also benefit from the specifics within this section. This section will be a major resource when all three readerships begin their journey to professionalism.

22

Your Evaluation Process

This chapter is targeted for all three intended readerships. Teacher education candidates will glean information that will assist them during their evaluations as an intern or student teacher. Alternative certification candidates and certified teachers in the field will learn tips to best assist them in this process. Every individual associated with the world of education is evaluated. This chapter views this process from the classroom teacher's perspective. Rather than "how to evaluate an individual," this chapter looks at "how to be the best prepared for my evaluation process."

Just as the student is continuously evaluated, so are the teachers. Due in part to the landmark report *A Nation at Risk* (1983), every aspect of schools has become more accountable through evaluations and assessments. Students, teachers, and administrators have specific goals and objectives that they must accomplish.

Your evaluation will be a process that spans the school year as opposed to an event that occurs once and is quickly over. The purpose of your evaluation process is multifaceted and can provide you with unique and individualized information regarding your professional qualifications. One purpose of your evaluation process is professional growth or professional evolution. I see teachers improve over the span of the school year just as I have seen students improve their skills during this time. Your conferences following the evaluation will provide you with many constructive suggestions, which can assist you in improving or enhancing specific areas. The evaluation process will promote reflective thinking on your part. You will be able to consider where you are and what you wish to become as a professional. Through reflective thinking, you can design a plan that will assist you to become more effective. By taking a proactive approach, you can evolve into a confident professional in your classroom and an asset to your district.

When training to become a public school administrator, I was taught to have a short conference with the new teachers at the site *prior* to evaluations. We were encouraged to provide them with a copy of the evaluation sheet, which had been approved by the board of education. The teacher should have an opportunity to ask questions *prior* to the evaluation process.

Before your administrator evaluates you, be certain that you know exactly what criteria will be used. If at all possible, receive a printed copy so you can double-check each item. Before scheduling an agreeable time for the administrator to visit for your evaluation, get answers to any questions you might have. Many administrators will want to set their schedule for evaluations without making the efforts to notify teachers regarding the evaluation criteria. It is to your advantage to learn the criteria in advance. As the university representative required to make evaluation visits to the classroom, I do not make my first visit until I have met with the teacher and gone over every aspect of the evaluation instrument. The teacher to be evaluated has ample opportunity to ask questions.

Every state has a different set of minimum criteria for evaluating teachers. The evaluation instrument used to evaluate teachers in Oklahoma has four categories: Human Relations, Teaching and Assessment, Classroom Management, and Professionalism. Each category has subtopics. For example, "Handles disruptive students effectively" is one subtopic under Classroom Management.

After you have learned the criteria for your evaluation, inquire specifically who will be evaluating you. Some schools have more than one administrator. Will the same individual evaluate you throughout the school year? Will they share these responsibilities? Some districts have peer evaluations. Will teachers working with the same subject matter or the same grade-level students be evaluating you? When it comes to your evaluation, assume nothing—ask everything.

After you have established who will be doing the evaluations, learn an approximate time frame for you to meet the objectives of the criteria. At the secondary level an evaluation generally lasts for a class period. The time duration of a class period generally ranges from forty to sixty minutes, depending on the district. Evaluation times vary greatly from primary grades to upper elementary grades. Know your time frame in advance and plan accordingly.

BEFORE YOUR TEACHER EVALUATION

Prior to your evaluation, take some time to look closely around your classroom as an evaluator would. If your classroom rules are posted at the back of the classroom and the students face the front of the classroom, how will the students be able to read the rules? If your classroom rules are typed in ten-point font, how will the students be able to read the rules? If your students sit in groups, pods, or teams that face different walls of the rooms, consider posting *four* sets of rules for all to view.

This preevaluation checklist will be helpful to you prior to your evaluation:

- Know who will evaluate you and the time frame for the evaluation.
- Know the components of your evaluation criteria.
- Make every effort for the room to be clean and orderly. Be sure the trash is off the floor.
- Do not plan an extraordinary lesson for your evaluation. Evaluators want to see life as usual in your classroom. Do not plan a cooperative group activity if you have not done one this year. Do not plan a science experiment if you have not done one this year. Your students will behave better and react better to their normal routine. You will feel most comfortable doing what you do every day.
- Be certain that your grade book and lesson plan books are up-to-date and abide by school policy. If you use an electronic grade book or plan book, print out the directions for your administrator to follow to personally check. A second option is to print a hard copy of your plans and grades for your evaluator to use as a reference.
- If you have a classroom calendar bulletin board, be certain that it is up-to-date. If it's the middle of the month, have the current month up and running on your calendar.
- Have your required visuals in plain view: class rules, disaster plans/policies, mission statement, playground rules, and so forth.
- Have your grade book *closed* to maintain student confidentiality. Have your lesson plan book *open* to the current page.

- Dress professionally every day, but especially on your evaluation day! Even if you are evaluated on "casual Friday," dress as you would on Thursday or Monday. This is a professional evaluation.
- If a videotaping process will be used with your evaluation, consider setting the equipment in place a few days in advance. The students will become used to the equipment being in the classroom. They will never know when the tape is rolling or stopped.

DURING YOUR TEACHER EVALUATION

When the evaluator is in place and you are ready to begin your evaluation, take one or two sentences to state what you did yesterday (or the last class meeting) and what you will be doing today. For example, "As you recall, yesterday we learned how to find the perimeter of a square. Today we are going to use a similar formula to find the perimeter of a rectangle." If you are beginning a new chapter, you might begin your lesson using this example, "You will remember in our last chapter we learned about the pilgrims preparing and making the journey to the New World. Today we will begin a new chapter in which we will learn about life in the Plymouth colony in a location that will become Massachusetts." In two sentences you have summarized the previous lesson or chapter and stated your teaching objective for today. Your students have been brought up to date. They have six or more subjects taught to them each day. The evaluator will be listening for some sort of introduction in which you state your objective or topic at the beginning of the lesson. If you do not state this information, the evaluator will sit through the entire lesson trying to figure out the objective.

The very first student teacher with whom I ever worked became one of my professional colleagues. I could stand outside her classroom and hear her introduce her lessons with the famous line, "As you recall , . . ." When I went into the field to serve as a university representative, every former student of mine *always* introduced his or her lesson in this fashion. As the evaluator, I found it so easy to listen to a few words and completely grasp the purpose of the lesson. As a professor of elementary education methods courses, I always encourage my students to begin *every* lesson in this way. If you cannot remember what the class studied yesterday in mathematics, ask a student. For example, "Susan, please share with the class what we studied in mathematics yesterday." Then state what they will be learning today.

Some suggestions to consider during your evaluation follow:

- Be aware of your movements. Some individuals tend to plant their feet in cement and stand glued to the podium during the lesson. Some individuals tend to roam all around the room in an exhausting fashion. Do not distract the students with your movements. Do not put them to sleep with your movements. Find a happy medium.
- Be aware of your language speed. Some individuals become nervous and talk so fast that it is difficult to understand them. Slow things down to a comfortable rate of speech.
- Maintain the status quo. Keep things as normal as possible. If the intercom or an unexpected guest interrupts you, react the way you would at any other time—graciously and professionally. If the fire alarm goes off, conduct a fire drill. Events interrupt our instruction of students on a daily or hourly basis. Deal with things and move on.
- Pick up your notes or teacher's edition and hold it where you are standing or while you are walking rather than constantly moving back to your desk or the podium to check it. Presenters use a "wireless mouse" with computer-assisted presentations. They do not have to continuously move in front of the screen to press the mouse. Use this "wireless" concept when you are teaching.
- If you are incorporating technology (laser disks, computer-assisted learning activities, a video or film) or visual aids such as an overhead transparency, have everything set up and ready to run before you begin the lesson. The technological equipment should be ready to start at the push of a button. Have the overhead projector focused. Have the screen pulled down in advance. Professionals would double-check this before they begin *any* lesson.
- If you are going to use the chalkboard or whiteboard, check prior to your evaluation to be certain that you have chalk or working markers.

AFTER YOUR TEACHING EVALUATION

After your evaluation, you will have a conference to receive feedback from the evaluator. The conference will be a private meeting between you and your evaluator. This follow-up phase of your evaluation process is vital for your improvement and continued professional growth. Take this opportunity to ask questions and if necessary take notes; therefore, take paper and pencil with you to the meeting. Your administrator may offer professional development opportunities to assist you in improving a deficient area or an area of interest. If you are in fact deficient in an area, learn specific ways in which you can improve. Keep suggestions in writing to alleviate any possible future communication problems or confusion.

CONCLUSION

Evaluations take all forms and shapes. Some districts incorporate student evaluations of the teacher as part of his or her evaluation. Some districts require a videotape lesson or lessons as part of the total evaluation process. In some districts, teachers are required to maintain a professional portfolio and include letters from students, parents, and colleagues. Peer and self-evaluations are also included in the evaluative process in some locations. As technology progresses, more and more innovations will be incorporated into the total package of teacher evaluations.

WEB REFERENCES

http://7-12educators.about.com/gi/dynamic/offsite.htm?site=http%3A%2F%2F
www.teachnet.com%2Fhow-to%2Forganization%2F092998.html. This website
provides checklists for teachers of English, science, and mathematics. Check out
this site prior to and after your evaluation.

http://www.ed.gov/pubs/NatAtRisk. Read more about *A Nation at Risk*, first released
in 1983, on this website.

http://edreform.com/pubs/manifest.htm. If you wish to see the progress America has
made as a result of *A Nation at Risk*, please see *A Nation Still at Risk: An Education
Manifesto* on this website released April 30, 1998.

23

Professional Portfolio

This chapter is designed for those teaching in the field today and also for those student teachers who will soon be in the rank and file of American educators. Teacher education candidates have strict portfolio requirements through their universities that must be followed to the letter. When they become teachers, they will have opportunities for options, choices, and creativity.

The purpose of a portfolio (according to the assessment section) is to show students' progress over time. Transferring that definition from students to teachers, the purpose of a professional portfolio is to show the teacher's professional progress over time. Obviously, if you have only been teaching a short time, your portfolio content will be much less than if you have been in the profession for years.

When beginning to create your professional portfolio, examine your options carefully. You could use the standard six-inch thick notebook like you used in your teacher education program. Get out those plastic sheets and begin the process! You may choose to create an e-portfolio. Utilize that digital camera, scanner, and all your computer software to the maximum capability. A third option is to begin with a tangible scrapbook form and then transfer your best work into a digital e-portfolio.

WHAT TO INCLUDE?

Whichever choice you make to compile your portfolio, you still must decide on the contents. You may wish to choose some rather untraditional items to add to your portfolio. Some old standards still need to be included in all portfolios, no matter what teaching assignment you may have. The following list includes possible items to include in your professional portfolio:

Relevant Professional Experience

- Include a chronological description of your teaching assignments by school year. You might want to add some additional information about your teaching assignments. For example, "During 1999–2000, I had one-third of my class enrollment with IEPs." This shows that you have had experience working with special needs students."
- Include your teaching certifications/credentials. List what you are certified to teach, specifying the state or states in which you hold that certification.
- Cite university data—years and locations where you attended college. With so many universities in the country, initials can be very confusing. OSU means Oklahoma State University to me; however, it could also mean Ohio State or Oregon State to others. Be specific. Include the dates and names of your degrees. For instance, "B.S. in social studies in 1997 from the University of Tulsa, Tulsa, Oklahoma."

Samples

- Samples of teaching units and assessments that you have created
- Set of classroom rules that you have designed
- Classroom mission statement

Communications

- Samples of class newsletters
- Any clippings about you or your class from school newspapers or local newspapers (use with permission)
- Samples of a progress report form that you have created to send home to parents
- Samples of parent–teacher conference forms that you have created

Professional Development

- Log with one- or two-sentence explanation of content for each workshop or program attended. Include dates. Specify if this was a district, county, state, or national meeting.
- Cooperation within the district—committee work
- Additional courses completed—list course title, university or college attended, and semester the course was completed. Some individuals may choose to include the transcript for verification.

Volunteer Work

- Volunteer work within the district
- Volunteer work within the community. You may choose to include volunteer work with religious or political organizations. Some individuals choose to delete this information from their portfolios; others choose to include it. This is *your* portfolio, so your choice.

Compliments

- Positive letters or notes from parents, students, and former students—be sure to include the date.
- Copies of favorable evaluations. Some professionals will be evaluated by only one individual; some will be evaluated by a team of individuals. You might include in this portion a short explanation of the number of evaluators and evaluations you have each year.

"Outside the Box" Category

- Consider the options available through technology. Include entries that provide auditory and visual information about you and your teaching.
- Pictures of you in action in your classroom—add narration for clarification.
- Auditory cassette tapes or VCR tapes of students' musical performances, debates, class plays, science fair projects, and so forth.
- Digital photos of class murals, field trip or fieldwork, and other special events or projects.

CONCLUSION

Portfolios show growth over time. Your professional portfolio will be a creative representation of your achievements as a professional.

REFERENCES

Tucker, P. D., J. H. Strong, and C. R. Gareis. 2002. *Handbook on teacher portfolios for evaluation and professional development.* Larchmont, N.Y.: Eye on Education. This book and CD-ROM are designed for both Macintosh and Windows users.

Wilcox, B. L., and L. A. Tomei. 1999. *Professional portfolios for teachers: A guide for learners, experts, and scholars with CD-ROM.* Norwood, Mass.: Christopher-Gordon. This book and CD-ROM cover the "transitional" development of teachers as they move through a career, recording a history of development, maturation, and professional achievement.

Fill in Your Gaps

Professional Development

Each district probably refers to this topic by a different name—*workshops, seminars,* or *staff development.* Whatever the name, it all falls under the umbrella "professional development." The purpose of these workshops, seminars, or staff development is to benefit you in your professional career. Every professional on the planet can benefit from professional development in some area.

As a teacher relatively new to the profession, you should attend any and all programs that will be of benefit to you and your students. Most districts will offer a variety of professional development opportunities. If this is not the case in your district, visit with your building principal about the possibility of attending professional development sessions in a specific area or discipline. Administrators have flyers come across their desks on a weekly basis. If they are aware of your desire to attend something specific, they will be looking for you.

Most districts or sites have a professional development coordinator. Make a point to know the name of this individual. If necessary, contact this person to notify them of your intentions to attend professional development offerings in a specific area. They will have the resources available to assist you.

Many states and/or districts have specific requirements regarding a specified number of hours of professional development required per year. Ask your faculty members or principal about the requirements in your district or state. Be certain that you have the required number of hours needed for professional development. Also be certain of your time frame in which the number

of hours must be accrued. The time frame might be from July 1 through June
30. If you are planning to attend special courses or workshops in the summer,
know in advance into which year your professional development hours will be
added.

Most districts in the United States have faculty members who are affiliated
with a professional organization. As a new teacher, ask your principal or a fellow teacher about the option of joining a professional organization. The following websites will be a wealth of knowledge and also provide you with links
to other areas. Valuable information is just a "click" away.

General
www.nea.org. Website for the National Educational Organization. You may
also check for information regarding your state educational organization.

www.aft.org. Website for the American Federation of Teachers.

Early Childhood
www.udel.edu/bateman/acei/. Website for the Association for Childhood
Education International (ACEI). Good site for early childhood teachers.

www.naeyc.org/default.htm. Website for National Association for the Education of Young Children. Good site for early childhood teachers.

Educational Technology
www.tmn.com/Organizatins/Iris/ITA.html. Website for the International
Technology Education Association.

English
www/ncte.org. Website for the National Council of English Teachers. This
site provides information about national and regional conferences as well
as many useful links.

ESL
www.tesol.org. Website for Teachers of English Speakers of Other Languages, Inc. Good source for teachers with ESL/LEP students in classes.

French
www.utsa.edu/aatf/aatf_fr.html. Website for the American Association of
Teachers of French (AATF).

Foreign Language

www.infi.net/~actfl/. Website for the American Council on the Teaching of Foreign Languages (ACTFK), a professional association that represents teachers of all languages at all educational levels.

Mathematics

www.nctm.org. Website for the National Council of Teachers of Mathematics. This site provides information about national and regional conferences as well as many useful links.

Music

www.electriciti.com/namm/opus/save_music_education.html. Website for the national Coalition for Music Education, whose motto is "Music for Every Child."

Physical Education

www.aahperd.org/naspt.html. Website for the National Association for Sport and Physical Education (NASPE), a national association devoted to improving the total sport and physical education experience in the United States.

Reading

www.reading.org. Website for the International Reading Association. This site offers information about national and international conferences as well as many useful links.

Science

www.nsta.org. Website for the National Science Teacher's Association. This site has information about national and regional conferences as well as many useful links.

Social Studies

www.ncss.org. Website for the National Council for the Social Studies. This site provides information about national and regional conferences as well as many useful links.

25

Sit Back and Shine

Your family consists of cherished members from a variety of age groups. You may be blessed to have two or three or perhaps even four or five generations within your family. Your school family also is a mosaic of cherished members referred to as faculty members. Some members of your school family were teaching before you were born! Some are young recruits like you. Some are parents juggling family responsibilities with their work schedule. Some are singles. Each piece of the puzzle is individualized and special in its own respect; however, when all the pieces come together, a fine-tuned, highly specialized faculty results.

You can learn management tips from one teacher and creative art ideas from another. It is your opportunity, rather than your responsibility, to go out there and learn the special gifts and talents of your fellow faculty members. Ask a zillion questions of everyone.

Just as other faculty members have areas in which they shine, so do you. If you are currently teaching in the field, you are the individual at your site with the current information regarding the newest trends and buzzwords. You know the most recent theory on teaching reading or math. You are well read and knowledgeable on so many current trends and philosophies in education today.

You also have a specialized area that can contribute to the faculty. It has been my experience that most recent graduates are light-years ahead of other teachers in the area of technology. Share your talents—any and all of them— with other faculty members. Rather than hide your talents under a bushel, as the children's song goes, "Let it shine, let it shine, let it shine!"

Now that you have completed this book, you are set for success. Take some time to carry out the suggestions from this book. Set up classroom rules, your lesson plan book and substitute folder, and your daily routine. Focus on the finite details at whatever point you are in the current school year. You will be able to sit back and enjoy your success for the remainder of the year. Keep notes and documentation for a great start for the following year.

It's never too late to roll up your sleeves and make some changes today to improve your classroom tomorrow. Consider areas of this book that can help you alleviate specific problems you are having. Pick and choose ways to help you save time and energy. You are a highly educated professional. You decide. Shine!

THE JOURNEY FROM TEACHER
TO PROFESSIONAL

PROFESSIONAL NETWORKING

As a newer teacher to the profession, you will be bombarded with so many things that are necessary and so many things that you want to do. Take some time to look around your school site and make note of the individuals who can be of special assistance to you.

The school librarian can be a wonderful resource. With advanced planning, the librarian can order videos, CDs, and library books to assist your students in learning a specific topic, such as oceanic mammals. Take some time to visit with the librarian to find out how much advance time he or she needs to order supplementary sources.

Another individual who can be invaluable to you is the special education teacher(s). If you have a student with an IEP, the special education teacher was on the IEP committee that wrote out the recommendations and modifications. You will be required by law to follow these recommendations and modifications. If you have any questions, schedule a meeting with the teacher and go over each aspect of the IEP. You will need to understand specifically what is expected of you. Also understand what assistance will or will not be provided by the special education teacher.

Your school site may have a remedial reading and/or remedial math program. Learn the requirements in order for students to qualify for one of these programs. Also find out how to refer your students for testing to this program as the year progresses. Some new teachers do not understand that children can be referred throughout the year.

Your school nurse is the "person to know." The nurse will assist in vision and hearing screenings. He or she will have some records regarding your students' medical histories. If you have a student with a disorder or condition that is completely new to you, such as obsessive compulsive disorder, the school nurse can find additional information to both inform and assist you to help this student attain the best education possible. The school nurse is also the person to contact when there is an outbreak of head lice in your classroom.

Most districts or sites have an individual responsible for professional development. This person will be a great resource to you. Take time to visit with the individual and express your interests in furthering your professional growth.

Your school counselor is a "gateway" individual. The counselor will know how students can be referred for testing ranging from the gifted program to special education. The counselor will most likely have the required forms for you to complete. If you have a student who might benefit from some form of additional testing, the counselor can find out whether and when the child was previously tested. Some districts have a policy specifying the number of times a student can be tested for a program. Use your counselor as a trusted resource to help you provide the best possible learning opportunities for your students.

About the Author

Linda Henshall Wilson, Ed. D., is a seasoned educator with experience at all levels of public school teaching as well as at the university level. A native Oklahoman, she has three degrees from Oklahoma State University, including a doctorate degree in education. She is an experienced and knowledgeable educator, speaker, and presenter whose career has spanned parts of four decades. Wilson brings a practical and applicable perspective to the contents of *Teaching 201: Traveling Beyond the Basics.* Presently she works with teacher education candidates and alternative certification candidates, as well as graduate students, at Langston University in Tulsa. She also works with first-year teachers and student teachers in northeastern Oklahoma.